P9-CLP-531

INTELLECTUAL ALIENATION IN THE 1920'S

PROBLEMS IN AMERICAN CIVILIZATION

INTELLECTUAL ALIENATION IN THE 1920'S

EDITED WITH AN INTRODUCTION BY

Milton Plesur

STATE UNIVERSITY OF NEW YORK AT BUFFALO

D. C. HEATH AND COMPANY

Lexington, Massachusetts

Printed in the United States of America

Library of Congress Number: 72–134279

ACKNOWLEDGMENTS

The author acknowledges with gratitude the assistance of the following during the time they were graduate assistants at the State University of New York at Buffalo: Dr. Douglas Frank, Mr. William J. Johnson, Dr. Carmen Notaro, Mr. Carl H. Perdue and Mr. Ross T. Runfola. Professor Selig Adler, Samuel Paul Capen Professor of American History at the State University of New York at Buffalo was, as usual, most helpful and cooperative in all phases of this work.

CONTENTS

INTRODUCTION

HISTORIANS and literary critics have been waging a battle since the nineteen-twenties over the relative merits of the writers of the "lost generation." According to some scholars and intellectuals, this group was both irresponsible and pernicious, while others are equally certain that they were the heralds of a cultural renaissance. Perhaps the only point on which the different factions agree is that the literature of the "jazz age" was quite different from that which preceded it. The issue is made all the more perplexing because it depends so heavily on personal perspectives and preferences. The facts do not speak for themselves; in this matter more than most others they must be interpreted.

The details of the case are deceptively simple. In the era immediately following the 1918 Armistice, a cadre of writers attacked the dominant values of American civilization. Most of them were entering young adulthood when the war began, and many of them became involved in the conflict as members of the military or ambulance drivers, or in some other noncombatant capacity. Virtually all were disillusioned with the Versailles peace machinery and equally disappointed at the current "Back to Normalcy" mood in the country.

One might argue that an assault upon American culture was not really a new departure for literature. The muckrakers of the preceding generation had established their reputations by uncovering abuses in various segments of society. Although the muckrakers were ruthless in their battle against social injustice, they rarely questioned the basic fabric of the society itself. Their aim was to eliminate the corruption of the few so that the underlying goodness of the many could prevail.

The alienated writers of the twenties, while equally distressed with the corruption and decay to be found in important sectors of government and business, carried their attack much further than the muckrakers. They struck at the heart of the nation itself; they directed their blows at the "common" man. Mediocrity was their target and the "average" American was their whipping boy. Critic H. L. Mencken was serious when he coined the phrase "Boobus Americanus" and he, and his devoted readers, applied it freely to the vast majority of their countrymen. The serious flaws that existed in American society, these critics held, could be placed squarely on the shoulders of the entire population. Americans were shortsighted, bigoted, intolerant, greedy and vain; and these terms applied not only to a few exploiters but to the herdlike masses.

Not all of the writers who are grouped together in the "disillusioned" category were as venomous as Mencken. Many of them saw the problem in a wider perspective, and they felt that the situation in America was no worse than in other parts of the Atlantic world. Some writers even found cause to be optimistic over the cultural possibilities that seemed to be evolving in this country. Although none were satisfied with the conditions prevalent at the time and all spoke out boldly for cultural change, no one but the unabashed Marxists demanded the destruction of the "Establishment," a perjorative term coined by a much later generation.

The controversy in this volume is centered primarily on the following issues: Was the American character accurately portrayed by these writers of the prosperity decade? Was this estimation socially responsible? Did the attack serve a significant cultural purpose or was it largely malicious and non-productive, as it subsequently proved to be in the case of Mencken?

The readings presented here in answer to these questions fall into two general categories. The first category is a presentation of the views of the writers themselves, while the second is a collection of critical essays that reflect the issues outlined in the preceding paragraph. Each category is further subdivided into sections which bring the critical questions into sharp focus and allow the reader to distinguish clearly between interpretive judgments.

The selections in the first group are not very optimistic in their appraisal of the American society of the 1920's. These are readings most likely to provoke controversy because of their highly critical content, and they are typical of those which will be discussed in detail by the critics in the subsequent selections.

The first example, from *This Side of Paradise* by F. Scott Fitzgerald, describes how the intellectual was being driven to disillusionment; how he experienced a sense of alienation.

The next selection is from Sinclair Lewis's *Main Street*. The issue here is the intolerance of fast-declining small-town America, and it touches indirectly on the intellectual and spiritual emptiness of contemporary religion. Attitudes toward sex and the double standard of morality also came under Lewis's fire, revealing the growing influence of Sigmund Freud on the American intellectual world.

In *Manhattan Transfer*, John Dos Passos criticizes social injustice and the lack of meaning and humanity in American culture. The selection included here deals with the rebellion of a young man when faced with some aspects of the impersonal business society which were particularly disgusting to him. In some respects it resembles the current dissatisfaction with the values and goals of a technological society.

Charles and Mary Beard depict the sense of alienation caused by the duplicity of the American government in entering World War I and in dealing with its aftermath. The Beards ascribe the cause of intellectual disillusionment to the Wilson administration, which led the United States into a war to make the world "safe for democracy," and then betrayed such high purposes by abusing that democracy in the "Red Scare" of the post-Armistice period.

From the vantage of an elitist view of culture, Irving Babbitt is critical of both America's emphasis on the quantity of material goods it has produced and its lack of standards. He also deplored the promotion of a standardized mediocrity, resulting in part from the inability of mass democracy to choose leaders of high caliber.

John Dewey's view that materialistic and artistic development must proceed together is presented in the next selection. The celebrated philosopher-educator is more optimistic than most of the other writers in this group, and he develops a good historical and logical foundation for his reasoning. He warns, however, that the future development of American society is intimately associated with the quality of the educational system. He points out that too little attention is being paid to social functions, while a preponderance of effort is expended on the technical aspects of society. Dewey pleads for a union of the aesthetic and the technical that will prevent society from becoming a technological monstrosity devoid of humanitarian meaning and beauty.

Walter Lippmann's description of Calvin Coolidge is a classic portrayal of the President's apparent mediocrity. He satirizes not only Coolidge, but also the people who elected him. Here again the target is not only the "incompetent" leaders but the nation of "blunderers" that sustains them.

The final selection from the writers of the nineteen-twenties is an essay by H. L. Mencken entitled, "The Democratic Citizen." Mencken deals with the repression of originality and vitality by American democracy and decries the democratic drone and emptiness of his surroundings. The "Sage of Baltimore" was worshipped by many intellectuals during the twenties, and he is merciless in his attack on the anti-intellectual segment of post-war society.

The next four essays address themselves to the question, "Can an artist exist and function freely in the United States?".[1] Mary Austin, the author of the first selection, optimistically discusses the rich potential of the American scene to provide exciting and vital material with which the artist could work. It was her belief that all that was needed in the United States was the presence of critics capable of recognizing good literature as it appeared.

In the next selection, Theodore Dreiser voices his opinion that America in the twenties was an improvement over preceding eras as far as tolerance for artistic work was concerned. Despite his radical temperament, he believed that the nation was no worse, and probably a good deal better, in artistic environment than other places were in other epochs.

Sherwood Anderson includes in his evaluation some of the points made by both Mary Austin and Theodore Dreiser. He then proceeds to take the "expatriates" to task, claiming there was nothing to be gained by their flight. He felt that there was a wealth of material in this country with which the artist could busy himself, and that by escaping abroad, he was only denying himself the opportunity for creativity on his native soil.

The final article in this group is by Zona Gale, the greatest Pollyanna included here. She felt that the task of the artist was to portray life realistically, not as one would like it to be. Humdrum existence in the United States, therefore, was as worthy of portrayal as life anywhere else. She was also convinced that the void in the realm of literary criticism in this country was finally being filled by top-notch talent. This made her confident that Americans would respond to the new impetus to excel in the arts.

The next three selections are grouped together because they were written by critics who shared the view that the writers of the twenties were neither accurate nor responsible, and their productions therefore contain faults that significantly impair their penetrations of the values of the era.

John W. Aldridge perceives the post-1918 years as a sharp, but not salutary, break with past literary traditions. The war, argues Aldridge, "infected [the writers] with irresponsibility" and made them "pursue pleasure with an intensity made greater by the constant threat of death." This sense of "spiritual emptiness" led them logically to conscious revolt in order to "sustain the emotions which the war had aroused in them." Life would always be perceived within the tragic framework of the war. In the end, the "deliberate exercise in futility" led to fanaticism and impotence in creativity. While the ideals fostered by the Great War produced a good literature and many excellent writers, Aldridge concludes "they were bad for life and they produced as many broken human beings."

Van Wyck Brooks, the next critic in this group, finds the literature of the 1920's wholly aberrant. While the dominant need in American writing has been "will, courage" and "faith in human nature," the authors of the decade "passively wallowed in misery, calling it fate." Instead of contributing to the good life, these artists accepted and embraced defeat, glorying in "enervation and disintegration." Writing as the clouds of war threatened America amidst the upheaval of Europe, Brooks hails the trend in the 1940's of a return to themes that would yield fruit from distinctively American roots.

The last of these critics is Bernard De Voto. In many respects he is probably the most effective of all in his criticism. Writing in 1944 with the havoc of World War II in full evidence, De Voto argues that it was not American civilization that was impoverished in the twenties, but the manner in which the *literati* thought about it. He condemns "the official literature" of the period, which he labeled as insignificant, because the intellectuals not only rejected our democratic ways but failed to recognize man's essential worth.

Directly opposed to the views of the

[1] This question was asked of a number of writers by *The Nation* in 1925. The selections that appear here were taken as representative samples from the replies offered by four of these *literati*.

previous critics stands another school which rates the writers of the twenties in much higher terms. Malcolm Cowley, focusing on the expatriates, believes that the post-war rebellion was merely a culmination of long-brewing passions. The revolt of the 1890's also expressed the feelings of an alienated generation. However ill-grounded the feeling of the writers of the 1920's that they were enjoying a unified experience, the exiles in Europe produced a literature that rejoined an older American tradition. Their style included a craft and precision which paralleled that of Hawthorne, Melville, or Henry James. Cowley concludes that the re-establishment of this earlier American tradition was "perhaps the most important result" of this adventure in exile.

Sharing Cowley's enthusiasm for the literary output of the twenties is Frederick J. Hoffman. Writing during the 1950's, Hoffman has a high regard for "jazz age" literature because of its new insight into our culture and its technical skill. He contends that the artist has a right to have a "private view of public affairs" and gives thanks for their "useful innocence" which allowed them to be concerned with aesthetic values. Critics like De Voto, who blame the writers of the 1920's for a loss of faith in democracy, fail to see that they were trying to create a new moral order based on these values. Hoffman contends that the intellectuals in the twenties renewed their culture by reconstructing it according to new principles and freshly acquired insights into human nature.

The last group of selections is much more balanced in their approach. Henry Steele Commager, the author of the first selection in this section, is sympathetic in tone but criticizes the intellectuals for their lack of direction and purpose. The bitter diatribes from the literature of the twenties were, in his opinion, "oblique and insidious" because the writers themselves "were uncomfortable rather than indignant, derisive rather than rebellious; their protest was personal and their estrangement private." Sinclair Lewis mirrors the age for Commager because "he was content with surface effects" and was not interested in probing deeper into the causes of things. However, in contrast to the negative view of De Voto, Commager asks, how was it possible that artists were deluded for two generations? "Perhaps it was that the novelists," he says in answer to this rhetorical question, "were idealists, that they took seriously the promise of American life, expected to realize the American dream."

The next critic is Arthur M. Schlesinger, Jr. In his view, the estrangement of the intellectuals began as a disenchantment with the business mentality and ended in an alienation from democracy itself. He describes Walter Lippmann's *A Preface to Morals* as a journey away from conviction, and goes on to discuss Joseph Wood Krutch's *The Modern Temper,* in which "mind itself had reasoned away, one by one, all those fixed points with reference to which life could be organized." Schlesinger is sympathetic but unconvinced that life was as bad as the writers of the twenties made it out to be.

Finally, the critic and erstwhile Communist, Granville Hicks, while sympathizing with the intellectuals in their loss of faith, finds most of them more pathetic than analytic. He says of Faulkner, "what it is he hates he scarcely knows," and he depicts T. S. Eliot as "feeble" and in need of the support offered by the High Anglicanism to which he turned. He similarly feels that Hemingway was close to the "point at which retreat becomes surrender and evasion becomes impotence." In John Dos Passos's work, however, he finds cause for optimism. He believes that Dos Passos has potential because he never surrendered to the gloom that so seriously affected the other members of his generation.

The importance for the historian in resolving the problem presented by these readings cannot be overestimated. Literature serves as an accurate barometer by which the historian can gauge the temper of his times. In dealing with the twenties, however, the question arises whether the literature of the period was an accurate reflection of life or if the literature itself was blighted. This question revolves around the corollaries of whether the literature represented a sharp break with the past, and if so, whether the break is to be commended. The resolution of these questions will determine whether or not the historian is justified in using the literary contributions of the 1920's as a tool in uncovering other aspects of the culture of that period.

CONFLICT OF OPINION

F. Scott Fitzgerald and Irving Babbitt viewed the discontent of some members of the intellectual community:

> Here was a new generation, . . . destined finally to go out into that dirty gray turmoil to follow love and pride; a new generation dedicated more than the last to the fear of poverty and the worship of success; grown up to find all Gods dead, all wars fought, all faiths in man shaken. . . .
>
> —F. SCOTT FITZGERALD

> One is inclined, indeed, to ask, in certain moods, whether the net result of the movement that has been sweeping the Occident for several generations may not be a huge mass of standardized mediocrity; and whether in this country in particular we are not in danger of producing in the name of democracy one of the most trifling brands of the human species that the world has yet seen.
>
> —IRVING BABBITT

Many writers felt that American society was not hostile to their artistic temperament:

> With all its defects, whatever they may be, social, religious, moral, I still cannot see that America so much more than any other country is lacking in those things which should stimulate or at least make bearable the life of an artist.
>
> —THEODORE DREISER

> The American who tries to escape by running off to live, say in Europe, is putting himself out of it altogether. To get at the story he has got to stay where the story is.
>
> —SHERWOOD ANDERSON

Literary critics also disagreed with the quality of American civilization prevailing during the twenties:

> I have remarked that for several years now literature has been confessing its errors. The confession of such an error as this is a confession of betrayal. It amounts to a confession that what truly was bankrupt was not American civilization but the literary way of thinking about it.
>
> —BERNARD DE VOTO

> Perhaps their strongest (at any rate their loudest) activity consisted of their documentation of human absurdities. This criticism of the modern world, in spite of its frequent triviality, was both a profound and a necessary contribution to the knowledge we must have of our society. We realize now that for the most part it was correct and shrewd.
>
> —FREDERICK J. HOFFMAN

Arthur M. Schlesinger, Jr., offers a synthesis to the central problem:

> What began as an alienation from business culture was ending in some cases as an alienation from democracy itself. And it was an alienation that provoked no exploration of social alternatives. . . . Never before in American history had artists and writers felt so impotent in their relation to American society. The business culture wanted nothing from the intellectual, had no use for him, gave him no sustenance.
>
> —ARTHUR M. SCHLESINGER, JR.

I. THE CRITICS AND DEFENDERS OF AMERICA IN THE 1920'S: THE INTELLECTUALS SPEAK FOR THEMSELVES

CRITICS

F. Scott Fitzgerald (1896–1940)

THIS SIDE OF PARADISE

F. Scott Fitzgerald was one of the best known postwar writers. His novels and short stories present a classic picture of the "jazz age." Fitzgerald's first book, *This Side of Paradise* (1920), expressed the rebellion of youth against the traditional values of their society in the 1920's. The following passage from that novel deals with the economic and political ideologies of the "lost generation," which were quite disturbing to the more conservative segments of society.

THE BIG MAN WITH GOGGLES

On the day that Amory started on his walk to Princeton the sky was a colorless vault, cool, high and barren of the threat of rain. It was a gray day, that least fleshly of all weathers; a day of dreams and far hopes and clear visions. It was a day easily associated with those abstract truths and purities that dissolve in the sunshine or fade out in mocking laughter by the light of the moon. The trees and clouds were carved in classical severity; the sounds of the countryside had harmonized to a monotone, metallic as a trumpet, breathless as the Grecian urn.

The day had put Amory in such a contemplative mood that he caused much annoyance to several motorists who were forced to slow up considerably or else run him down. So engrossed in his thoughts was he that he was scarcely surprised at that strange phenomenon—cordiality manifested within fifty miles of Manhattan—when a passing car slowed down beside him and a voice hailed him. He looked up and saw a magnificent Locomobile in which sat two middle-aged men, one of them small and anxious looking, apparently an artificial growth on the other who was large and begoggled and imposing.

"Do you want a lift?" asked the apparently artificial growth, glancing from the corner of his eye at the imposing man as if for some habitual, silent corroboration.

"You bet I do. Thanks."

The chauffeur swung open the door, and, climbing in, Amory settled himself in the middle of the back seat. He took in his companions curiously. The chief characteristic of the big man seemed tc be a great confidence in himself set off against a tremendous boredom with everything around him. That part of his face which protruded under the goggles was what is generally termed "strong"; rolls of not undignified fat had collected near his chin; somewhere above was a wide thin mouth and the rough model for a Roman nose, and, below, his shoulders collapsed without a struggle into the powerful bulk of his chest and belly. He was excellently and quietly dressed. Amory noticed that he was inclined to stare straight at the back of the chauffeur's head as if speculating steadily but hopelessly some baffling hirsute problem.

The smaller man was remarkable only for his complete submersion in the personality of the other. He was of that lower secretarial type who at forty have engraved upon their business cards: "Assistant to the President," and without a sigh consecrate the rest of their lives to second-hand mannerisms.

"Going far?" asked the smaller man in a pleasant disinterested way.

"Quite a stretch."

"Hiking for exercise?"

"No," responded Amory succinctly, "I'm walking because I can't afford to ride."

"Oh."

Then again:

"Are you looking for work? Because there's lots of work," he continued rather testily. "All this talk of lack of work. The West is especially short of labor." He expressed the West with a sweeping, lateral gesture. Amory nodded politely.

"Have you a trade?"

No—Amory had no trade.

"Clerk, eh?"

No—Amory was not a clerk.

"Whatever your line is," said the little man, seeming to agree wisely with something Amory had said, "now is the time of opportunity and business openings." He glanced again toward the big man, as a lawyer grilling a witness glances involuntarily at the jury.

Amory decided that he must say something and for the life of him could think of only one thing to say.

"Of course I want a great deal of money——"

The little man laughed mirthlessly but conscientiously.

"That's what every one wants nowadays, but they don't want to work for it."

"A very natural, healthy desire. Almost all normal people want to be rich without great effort—except the financiers in problems plays, who want to 'crash their way through.' Don't you want easy money?"

"Of course not," said the secretary indignantly.

"But," continued Amory disregarding him, "being very poor at present I am contemplating socialism as possibly my forte."

Both men glanced at him curiously.

"These bomb throwers—" The little man ceased as words lurched ponderously from the big man's chest.

"If I thought you were a bomb thrower I'd run you over to the Newark jail. That's what I think of Socialists."

Amory laughed.

"What are you," asked the big man, "one of these parlor Bolsheviks, one of these idealists? I must say I fail to see the difference. The idealists loaf around and write the stuff that stirs up the poor immigrants."

"Well," said Amory, "if being an idealist is both safe and lucrative, I might try it."

"What's your difficulty? Lost your job?"

"Not exactly, but—well, call it that."

"What was it?"

"Writing copy for an advertising agency."

"Lots of money in advertising."

Amory smiled discreetly.

"Oh, I'll admit there's money in it eventually. Talent doesn't starve any more. Even art gets enough to eat these days. Artists draw your magazine covers, write your advertisements, hash out rag-time for your theatres. By the great commercializing of printing you've found a harmless, polite occupation for every genius who might have carved his own niche. But beware the artist who's an intellectual also. The artist who doesn't fit—the Rousseau, the Tolstoi, the Samuel Butler, the Amory Blaine——"

"Who's he?" demanded the little man suspiciously.

"Well," said Amory, "he's a—he's an intellectual personage not very well known at present."

The little man laughed his conscientious laugh, and stopped rather suddenly as Amory's burning eyes turned on him.

"What are you laughing at?"

"These *intellectual* people——"

"Do you know what it means?"

The little man's eyes twitched nervously.

"Why, it *usually* means——"

"It *always* means brainy and well-educated," interrupted Amory. "It means having an active knowledge of the race's experience." Amory decided to be very rude. He turned to the big man. "The young man," he indicated the secretary with his thumb, and said young man as one says bell-boy, with no implication of youth, "has the usual muddled connotation of all popular words."

"You object to the fact that capital controls printing?" said the big man, fixing him with his goggles.

"Yes—and I object to doing their mental work for them. It seemed to me that the root of all the business I saw around me consisted in overworking and underpaying a bunch of dubs who submitted to it."

"Here now," said the big man, "you'll have to admit that the laboring man is certainly highly paid—five and six hour days—it's ridiculous. You can't buy an honest day's work from a man in the trade-unions."

"You've brought it on yourselves," insisted Amory. "You people never make concessions until they're wrung out of you."

"What people?"

"Your class; the class I belonged to until recently; those who by inheritance or industry or brains or dishonesty have become the moneyed class."

"Do you imagine that if that road-mender over there had the money he'd be any more willing to give it up?"

"No, but what's that got to do with it?"

The older man considered.

"No, I'll admit it hasn't. It rather sounds as if it had though."

"In fact," continued Amory, "he'd be worse. The lower classes are narrower, less pleasant and personally more selfish—certainly more stupid. But all that has nothing to do with the question."

"Just exactly what is the question?"

Here Amory had to pause to consider exactly what the question was.

AMORY COINS A PHRASE

"When life gets hold of a brainy man of fair education," began Amory slowly, "that is, when he marries he becomes, nine times out of ten, a conservative as far as existing social conditions are concerned. He may be unselfish, kind-hearted, even just in his own way, but his first job is to provide and to hold fast. His wife shoos him on, from ten thousand a year to twenty thousand a year, on and on, in an enclosed treadmill that hasn't any windows. He's done! Life's got him! He's no help! He's a spiritually married man."

Amory paused and decided that it wasn't such a bad phrase.

"Some men," he continued, "escape the grip. Maybe their wives have no social ambitions; maybe they've hit a sentence or two in a 'dangerous book' that pleased them; maybe they started on the treadmill as I did and were knocked off. Anyway, they're the congressmen you can't bribe, the Presidents who aren't politicians, the writers, speakers, scientists, statesmen who aren't just popular grab-bags for a half-dozen women and children."

"He's the natural radical?"

"Yes," said Amory. "He may vary from the disillusioned critic like old Thorton Hancock, all the way to Trotsky. Now this spiritually unmarried man hasn't direct power, for unfortunately the spiritually married man, as a by-product of his money chase, has garnered in the great newspaper, the popular magazine, the influential weekly—so that Mrs. Newspaper, Mrs. Magazine, Mrs. Weekly can have a better limousine than those oil people across the street or those cement people 'round the corner."

"Why not?"

"It makes wealthy men the keepers of the world's intellectual conscience and, of course, a man who has money under one set of social institutions quite naturally can't risk his family's happiness by letting the clamor for another appear in his newspaper."

"But it appears," said the big man.

"Where?—in the discredited mediums. Rotten cheap-papered weeklies."

"All right—go on."

"Well, my first point is that through a mixture of conditions of which the family is the first, there are these two sorts of brains. One sort takes human nature as it finds it, uses its timidity, its weakness, and its strength for its own ends. Opposed is the man who, being spiritually unmarried, continually seeks for new systems that will control or counteract human nature. His problem is harder. It is not life that's complicated, it's the struggle to guide and control life. That is his struggle. He is a part of progress—the spiritually married man is not."

The big man produced three big cigars, and proffered them on his huge palm. The little man took one, Amory shook his head and reached for a cigarette.

"Go on talking," said the big man. "I've been wanting to hear one of you fellows."

GOING FASTER

"Modern life," began Amory again, "changes no longer century by century, but year by year, ten times faster than it ever has before—populations doubling, civilizations unified more closely with other civilizations, economic interdependence, racial questions, and—we're *dawdling* along. My idea is that we've got to go very much faster." He slightly emphasized the last words and the chauffeur unconsciously increased the speed of the car. Amory and the big man laughed; the little man laughed, too, after a pause.

"Every child," said Amory, "should have an equal start. If his father can endow him with a good physique and his mother with some common sense in his early education, that should be his heritage. If the father can't give him a good physique, if the mother has spent in chasing men the years in which she should have been preparing herself to educate her children, so much the worse for the child. He shouldn't be artificially bolstered up with money, sent to these horrible tutoring schools, dragged through college . . . Every boy ought to have an equal start."

"All right," said the big man, his goggles indicating neither approval nor objection.

"Next I'd have a fair trial of government ownership of all industries."

"That's been proven a failure."

"No—it merely failed. If we had government ownership we'd have the best analytical business minds in the government working for something besides themselves. We'd have Mackays instead of Burlesons; we'd have Morgans in the Treasury Department; we'd have Hills running interstate commerce. We'd have the best lawyers in the Senate."

"They wouldn't give their best efforts for nothing. McAdoo——"

"No," said Amory, shaking his head. "Money isn't the only stimulus that brings out the best that's in a man, even in America."

"You said a while ago that it was."

"It is, right now. But if it were made illegal to have more than a certain amount the best men would all flock for the one other reward which attracts humanity—honor."

The big man made a sound that was very like *boo*.

"That's the silliest thing you've said yet."

"No, it isn't silly. It's quite plausible. If you'd gone to college you'd have been struck by the fact that the men there would work twice as hard for any one of a hundred petty honors as those other men did who were earning their way through."

"Kids—child's play!" scoffed his antagonist.

"Not by a darned sight—unless we're all children. Did you ever see a grown man when he's trying for a secret society—or a rising family whose name is up at some club? They'll jump when they hear the sound of the word. The idea that to make a man work you've got to hold gold in front of his eyes is a growth, not an axiom. We've done that for so long that we've forgotten there's any other way. We've made a world where that's necessary. Let me tell you"— Amory became emphatic—"if there were ten men insured against either wealth or starvation, and offered a green ribbon for five hours' work a day and a blue ribbon for ten hours' work a day, nine out of ten of them would be trying for the blue ribbon. That competitive instinct only wants a badge. If the size of their house is the badge they'll sweat their heads off for that. If it's only a blue ribbon, I damn near believe they'll work just as hard. They have in other ages."

"I don't agree with you."

"I know it," said Amory nodding sadly. "It doesn't matter any more though. I think these people are going to come and take what they want pretty soon."

A fierce hiss came from the little man. *"Machine-guns!"*

"Ah, but you've taught them their use."

The big man shook his head.

"In this country there are enough property owners not to permit that sort of thing."

Amory wished he knew the statistics of property owners and non-property owners; he decided to change the subject.

But the big man was aroused.

"When you talk of 'taking things away,' you're on dangerous ground."

"How can they get it without taking it? For years people have been stalled off with promises. Socialism may not be progress, but the threat of the red flag is certainly the inspiring force of all reform. You've got to be sensational to get attention."

"Russia is your example of a beneficent violence, I suppose?"

"Quite possibly," admitted Amory. "Of course, it's overflowing just as the French Revolution did, but I've no doubt that it's really a great experiment and well worth while."

"Don't you believe in moderation?"

"You won't listen to the moderates, and it's almost too late. The truth is that the public has done one of those startling and amazing things that they do about once in a hundred years. They've seized an idea."

"What is it?"

"That however the brains and abilities of men may differ, their stomachs are essentially the same." . . .

OUT OF THE FIRE, OUT OF THE LITTLE ROOM

Eight hours from Princeton Amory sat down by the Jersey roadside and looked at the frost-bitten country. Nature as a rather coarse phenomenon composed largely of flowers that, when closely inspected, appeared motheaten, and of ants that endlessly traversed blades of grass, was always disillusioning; nature represented by skies and waters and far horizons was more likable. Frost and the promise of winter thrilled him now, made him think of a wild battle between St. Regis and Groton, ages ago, seven years ago—and of an autumn day in France twelve months before when he had lain in tall grass, his platoon flattened down close around him, waiting to tap the shoulders of a Lewis gunner. He saw the two pictures together with somewhat the same primitive exaltation—two games he had played, differing in quality of acerbity, linked in a way that differed them from Rosalind or the subject of labyrinths which were, after all, the business of life.

"I am selfish," he thought.

"This is not a quality that will change when I 'see human suffering' or 'lose my parents' or 'help others.'

"This selfishness is not only part of me. It is the most living part.

"It is by somehow transcending rather than by avoiding that selfishness that I can bring poise and balance into my life.

"There is no virtue of unselfishness that I cannot use. I can make sacrifices, be charitable, give to a friend, endure for a friend, lay down my life for a friend—all because these things may be the best possible expression of myself; yet I have not one drop of the milk of human kindness."

The problem of evil had solidified for Amory into the problem of sex. He was beginning to identify evil with the strong phallic worship in Brooke and the early Wells. Inseparably linked with evil was beauty—beauty, still a constant rising tumult; soft in Eleanor's voice, in an old song at night, rioting deliriously through life like superimposed waterfalls, half rhythm, half darkness. Amory knew that every time he had reached toward it longingly it had leered out at him with the grotesque face of evil. Beauty of great art, beauty of all joy, most of all the beauty of women.

After all, it had too many associations with license and indulgence. Weak things were often beautiful, weak things were never good. And in this new loneliness of his that had been selected for what greatness he might achieve, beauty must be relative or, itself a harmony, it would make only a discord.

In a sense this gradual renunciation of beauty was the second step after his disillusion had been made complete. He felt that he was leaving behind him his chance of being a certain type of artist. It seemed so much more important to be a certain sort of man.

His mind turned a corner suddenly and he found himself thinking of the Catholic Church. The idea was strong in him that there was a certain intrinsic lack in those to whom orthodox religion was necessary, and religion to Amory meant the Church of Rome. Quite conceivably it was an empty ritual but it was seemingly the only assimilative, traditionary bulwark against the decay of morals. Until the great mobs could be educated into a moral sense some one must cry: "Thou shalt not!" Yet any acceptance was, for the present, impossible. He wanted time and the absence of ulterior pressure. He wanted to keep the tree without ornaments, realize fully the direction and momentum of this new start.

The afternoon waned from the purging good of three o'clock to the golden beauty of four. Afterward he walked through the dull ache of a setting sun when even the clouds seemed bleeding and at twilight he came to a graveyard. There was a dusky, dreamy smell of flowers and the ghost of a new moon in the sky and shadows everywhere. On an impulse he considered trying to open the door of a rusty iron vault built into the side of a hill; a vault washed clean and covered with late-blooming, weepy watery-blue flowers that might have grown from dead eyes, sticky to the touch with a sickening odor.

Amory wanted to *feel* "William Dayfield, 1864."

He wondered that graves ever made people consider life in vain. Somehow he could find nothing hopeless in having lived. All the broken columns and clasped hands and doves and angels meant romances. He fancied that in a hundred years he would like having young people speculate as to whether his eyes were brown or blue, and he hoped quite passionately that his grave would have about it an air of many, many years ago. It seemed strange that out of a row of Union soldiers two or three made him think of dead loves and dead lovers, when they were exactly like the rest, even to the yellowish moss.

Long after midnight the towers and spires of Princeton were visible, with here and there a late-burning light—and suddenly out of the clear darkness the sound of bells. As an endless dream it went on; the spirit of the past brooding over a new generation, the chosen youth from the muddled, unchastened world, still fed romantically on the mistakes and half-forgotten dreams of dead statesmen and poets. Here was a new generation, shouting the old cries, learning the old creeds, through a revery of long days and nights; destined finally to go out into that dirty gray turmoil to follow love and pride; a new generation dedicated more than the last to the fear of poverty and the worship of success;

grown up to find all Gods dead, all wars fought, all faiths in man shaken. . . .

Amory, sorry for them, was still not sorry for himself—art, politics, religion, whatever his medium should be, he knew he was safe now, free from all hysteria—he could accept what was acceptable, roam, grow, rebel, sleep deep through many nights. . . .

There was no God in his heart, he knew; his ideas were still in riot; there was ever the pain of memory; the regret for his lost youth—yet the waters of disillusion had left a deposit on his soul, responsibility and a love of life, the faint stirring of old ambitions and unrealized dreams. But—oh, Rosalind! Rosalind! . . .

"It's all a poor substitute at best," he said sadly.

And he could not tell why the struggle was worth while, why he had determined to use to the utmost himself and his heritage from the personalities he had passed. . . .

He stretched out his arms to the crystalline, radiant sky.

"I know myself," he cried, "but that is all."

Sinclair Lewis (1885–1951)

MAIN STREET

Sinclair Lewis, the first American to win the Nobel Prize (1930) for literature, was born and raised in Sauk Centre, Minnesota. In 1920, after several years of literary obscurity, he came into his own with *Main Street,* which was based on small town life. This excerpt from *Main Street* reveals religious bigotry and sexual prudishness of provincial America to which Lewis so strongly objected.

SHE was at Sunday morning service at the Baptist Church, in a solemn row with her husband, Hugh, Uncle Whittier, Aunt Bessie.

Despite Aunt Bessie's nagging the Kennicotts rarely attended church. The doctor asserted, "Sure, religion is a fine influence—got to have it to keep the lower classes in order—fact, it's the only thing that appeals to a lot of those fellows and makes 'em respect the rights of property. And I guess this theology is O.K.; lot of wise old coots figured it all out, and they knew more about it than we do." He believed in the Christian religion, and never thought about it; he believed in the church, and seldom went near it; he was shocked by Carol's lack of faith, and wasn't quite sure what was the nature of the faith that she lacked.

Carol herself was an uneasy and dodging agnostic.

When she ventured to Sunday School and heard the teachers droning that the genealogy of Shamsherai was a valuable ethical problem for children to think about; when she experimented with Wednesday prayer-meeting and listened to store-keeping elders giving their unvarying weekly testimony in primitive erotic symbols and such gory Chaldean phrases as "washed in the blood of the lamb" and "a vengeful God"; when Mrs. Bogart boasted that through his boyhood she had made Cy confess nightly upon the basis of the Ten Commandments; then Carol was dismayed to find the Christian religion, in America, in the twentieth century, as abnormal as Zoroastrianism—without the splendor. But when she went to church suppers and felt the friendliness, saw the gaiety with which the sisters served cold ham and scalloped potatoes; when Mrs. Champ Perry cried to her, on an afternoon call, "My dear, if you just knew how happy it makes you to come into abiding grace," then Carol found the humanness behind the sanguinary and alien theology. Always she perceived that the churches—Methodist, Baptist, Congregational, Catholic, all of them—which had seemed so unimportant to the judge's home in her childhood, so isolated from the city struggle in St. Paul, were still, in Gopher Prairie, the strongest of the forces compelling respectability.

This August Sunday she had been tempted by the announcement that the Reverend Edmund Zitterel would preach on the topic "America, Face Your Problems!" With the great war, workmen in every nation showing a desire to control industries, Russia hinting a leftward revolution against Kerensky, woman suffrage coming, there seemed to be plenty of problems for the Reverend Mr. Zitterel to call on America to face. Carol gathered her family and trotted off behind Uncle Whittier.

The congregation faced the heat with informality. Men with highly plastered hair, so painfully shaved that their faces looked sore, removed their coats, sighed, and unbuttoned two buttons of their uncreased Sunday vests. Large-bosomed, white-bloused, hot-necked, spectacled matrons—the Mothers in Israel, pioneers and friends of Mrs. Champ Perry—waved their palm-leaf fans in a steady rhythm. Abashed boys slunk into the rear pews and giggled, while milky little girls, up front with their mothers, self-consciously kept from turning around.

The church was half barn and half Gopher Prairie parlor. The streaky brown wallpaper was broken in its dismal sweep only by framed texts, "Come unto Me" and "The Lord Is My Shepherd," by a list of hymns, and by a crimson and green diagram, staggeringly drawn upon hemp-colored paper, indicating the alarming ease with which a young man may descend from Palaces of Pleasure and the House of Pride to Eternal Damnation. But the varnished oak pews and the new red carpet and the three large chairs on the platform, behind the bare reading-stand, were all of a rocking-chair comfort.

Carol was civic and neighborly and commendable today. She beamed and bowed. She trolled out with the others the hymn:

How pleasant 'tis on Sabbath morn
To gather in the church,
And there I'll have no carnal thoughts,
Nor sin shall me besmirch.

With a rustle of starched linen skirts and stiff shirt-fronts, the congregation sat down, and gave heed to the Reverend Mr. Zitterel. The priest was a thin, swart, intense young man with a bang. He wore a black sack suit and a lilac tie. He smote the enormous Bible on the reading-stand, vociferated, "Come, let us reason together," delivered a prayer informing Almighty God of the news of the past week, and began to reason.

It proved that the only problems which America had to face were Mormonism and Prohibition:

"Don't let any of these self-conceited fellows that are always trying to stir up trouble deceive you with the belief that there's anything to all these smart-aleck movements to let the unions and the Farmers' Nonpartisan League kill all our initiative and enterprise by fixing wages and prices. There isn't any movement that amounts to a whoop without it's got a moral background. And let me tell you that while folks are fussing about what they call 'economics' and 'socialism' and 'science' and a lot of things that are nothing in the world but a disguise for atheism, the Old Satan is busy spreading his secret net and tentacles out there in Utah, under his guise of Joe Smith or Brigham Young or whoever their leaders happen to be today, it doesn't make any difference, and they're making game of the Old Bible that has led this American people through its manifold trials and tribulations to its firm position as the fulfilment of the prophecies and the recognized leader of all nations. 'Sit thou on my right hand till I make thine enemies the footstool of my feet,' said the Lord of Hosts, Acts II, the thirty-fourth verse—and let me tell you right now, you got to get up a good deal earlier in the morning than you get up even when you're going fishing, if you want to be smarter than the Lord, who has shown us the straight and narrow way, and he that passeth therefrom is in eternal peril and, to return to this vital and terrible subject of Mormonism—and as I say, it is terrible to realize how little attention is given to this evil right here in our midst and on our very doorstep, as it were—it's a shame and a disgrace that the Congress of these United States spends all its time talking about inconsequential financial matters that ought to be left to the Treasury Department, as I understand it, instead of arising in their might and passing a law that any one admitting he is a Mormon shall simply be deported and as it were kicked out of this free country in which we haven't got any room for polygamy and the tyrannies of Satan.

"And, to digress for a moment, especially as there are more of them in this state than there are Mormons, though you never can tell what will happen with this vain generation of young girls, that think more about wearing silk stockings than about minding their mothers and learning to bake a good loaf of bread, and many of them listening to these sneaking Mormon missionaries—and I actually heard one of them talking right out on a street-corner in Duluth, a few years ago, and the officers of the law not protesting—but still, as they are a smaller but more immediate problem, let me stop for just a moment to pay my respects to these Seventh-Day Adventists. Not that they are immoral, I don't mean, but when a body of men go on insisting that Saturday is the Sabbath, after Christ himself has clearly indicated the new dispensation, then I think the legislature ought to step in——" . . .

Carol was on the back porch, tightening a bolt on the baby's go-cart, this Sunday afternoon. Through an open window of the Bogart house she heard a screeching, heard Mrs. Bogart's haggish voice:

". . . did too, and there's no use your denying it . . . no you don't, you march yourself right straight out of the house . . . never in my life heard of such . . . never had nobody talk to me like . . . walk in the ways of sin and nastiness . . . leave your clothes here, and heaven knows that's more than you deserve . . . any of your lip or I'll call the policeman."

The voice of the other interlocutor Carol did not catch, nor, though Mrs. Bogart was proclaiming that he was her confidant and present assistant, did she catch the voice of Mrs. Bogart's God.

"Another row with Cy," Carol inferred.

She trundled the go-cart down the back steps and tentatively wheeled it across the yard, proud of her repairs. She heard steps on the sidewalk. She saw not Cy Bogart but Fern Mullins, carrying a suit-case, hurrying up the street with her head low. The widow, standing on the porch with buttery arms akimbo, yammered after the fleeing girl:

"And don't you dare show your face on this block again. You can send the drayman for your trunk. My house has been contaminated long enough. Why the Lord should afflict me——"

Fern was gone. The righteous widow glared, banged into the house, came out poking at her bonnet, marched away. By this time Carol was staring in a manner not visibly to be distinguished from the window-peeping of the rest of Gopher Prairie. She saw Mrs. Bogart enter the Howland house, then the Casses'. Not till suppertime did she reach the Kennicotts. The doctor answered her ring, and greeted her. "Well, well, how's the good neighbor?"

The good neighbor charged into the living-room, waving the most unctuous of black kid gloves and delightedly sputtering:

"You may well ask how I am! I really do wonder how I could go through the awful scenes of this day—and the impudence I took from that woman's tongue, that ought to be cut out——"

"Whoa! Whoa! Hold up!" roared Kennicott. "Who's the hussy, Sister Bogart? Sit down and take it cool and tell us about it."

"I can't sit down, I must hurry home, but I couldn't devote myself to my own selfish cares till I'd warned you, and heaven knows I don't expect any thanks for trying to warn the town against her, there's always so much evil in the world that folks simply won't see or appreciate your trying to safeguard them—— And forcing herself in here to get in with you and Carrie, many's the time I've seen her doing it, and, thank heaven, she was found out in time before she could do any more harm, it simply breaks my heart and prostrates me to think what she may have done already, even if some of us that understand and know about things——"

"Whoa-up! Who are you talking about?"

"She's talking about Fern Mullins," Carol put in, not pleasantly.

"Huh?"

Kennicott was incredulous.

"I certainly am!" flourished Mrs. Bogart, "and good and thankful you may be that I found her out in time, before she could get *you* into something, Carol; because even if you are my neighbor and Will's wife and a cultured lady, let me tell you right now, Carol Kennicott, that you ain't always as respectful to—you ain't as reverent—you don't stick by the good old ways like they was laid down for us by God in the Bible, and while of course there ain't a bit of harm in having a good laugh, and I know there ain't any real wickedness in you, yet just the same you don't fear God and hate the transgressors of his commandments like you ought to, and you may be thankful I found out this serpent I nourished in my bosom—and oh yes! oh yes indeed! my lady must have two eggs every morning for breakfast, and eggs sixty cents a dozen, and wa'n't satisfied with one, like most folks —what did she care how much they cost or if a person couldn't make hardly nothing on her board and room, in fact I just took her in out of charity and I might have known from the kind of stockings and clothes that she sneaked into my house in her trunk——"

Before they got her story she had five more minutes of obscene wallowing. The gutter comedy turned into high tragedy, with Nemesis in black kid gloves. The actual story was simple, depressing, and unimportant. As to details Mrs. Bogart was indefinite, and angry that she should be questioned.

Fern Mullins and Cy had, the evening before, driven alone to a barn-dance in the country. (Carol brought out the admission that Fern had tried to get a chaperon). At the dance Cy had kissed Fern—she confessed that. Cy had obtained a pint of whisky; he said that he didn't remember where he had got it; Mrs. Bogart implied that Fern had given it to him; Fern herself insisted that he had stolen it from a farmer's overcoat—which, Mrs. Bogart raged, was obviously a lie. He had become soggily drunk. Fern had driven him home; deposited him, retching and wabbling, on the Bogart porch.

Never before had her boy been drunk, shrieked Mrs. Bogart. When Kennicott grunted, she owned, "Well, maybe once or twice I've smelled licker on his breath." She also, with an air of being only too scrupulously exact, granted that sometimes he did not come home till morning. But he couldn't ever have been drunk, for he always had the best excuses: the other boys had tempted him to go down the lake spearing pickerel by torchlight, or he had been out in a "machine that ran out of gas." Anyway, never before had her boy fallen into the hands of a "designing woman."

"What do you suppose Miss Mullins could design to do with him?" insisted Carol.

Mrs. Bogart was puzzled, gave it up, went on. This morning, when she had faced both of them, Cy had manfully confessed that all of the blame was on Fern, because the teacher—his own teacher—had dared him to take a drink. Fern had tried to deny it.

"Then," gabbled Mrs. Bogart, "then

that woman had the impudence to say to me, 'What purpose could I have in wanting the filthy pup to get drunk?' That's just what she called him—pup. 'I'll have no such nasty language in my house,' I says, 'and you pretending and pulling the wool over people's eyes and making them think you're educated and fit to be a teacher and look out for young people's morals—you're worse 'n any street-walker!' I says. I let her have it good. I wa'n't going to flinch from my bounden duty and let her think that decent folks had to stand for her vile talk. 'Purpose?' I says, 'Purpose? I'll tell you what purpose you had! Ain't I seen you making up to everything in pants that'd waste time and pay attention to your impert'nence? Ain't I seen you showing off your legs with them short skirts of yours, trying to make out like you was so girlish and la-de-da, running along the street?' "

Carol was very sick at this version of Fern's eager youth, but she was sicker as Mrs. Bogart hinted that no one could tell what had happened between Fern and Cy before the drive home. Without exactly describing the scene, by her power of lustful imagination the woman suggested dark country places apart from the lanterns and rude fiddling and banging dance-steps in the barn, then madness and harsh hateful conquest. Carol was too sick to interrupt. It was Kennicott who cried, "Oh, for God's sake quit it! You haven't any idea what happened. You haven't given us a single proof yet that Fern is anything but a rattle-brained youngster."

"I haven't, eh? Well, what do you say to this? I come straight out and I says to her, 'Did you or did you not taste the whisky Cy had?' and she says, 'I think I did take one sip—Cy made me,' she said. She owned up to that much, so you can imagine——"

"Does that prove her a prostitute?" asked Carol.

"Carrie! Don't you never use a word like that again!" wailed the outraged Puritan.

"Well, does it prove her to be a bad woman, that she took a taste of whisky? I've done it myself!"

"That's different. Not that I approve your doing it. What do the Scriptures tell us? 'Strong drink is a mocker!' But that's entirely different from a teacher drinking with one of her own pupils."

"Yes, it does sound bad. Fern was silly, undoubtedly. But as a matter of fact she's only a year or two older than Cy, and probably a good many years younger in experience of vice."

"That's—not—true! She is plenty old enough to corrupt him!"

"The job of corrupting Cy was done by your sinless town, five years ago!"

Mrs. Bogart did not rage in return. Suddenly she was hopeless. Her head drooped. She patted her black kid gloves, picked at a thread of her faded brown skirt, and sighed, "He's a good boy, and awful affectionate if you treat him right. Some thinks he's terrible wild, but that's because he's young. And he's so brave and truthful—why, he was one of the first in town that wanted to enlist for the war, and I had to speak real sharp to him to keep him from running away. I didn't want him to get into no bad influences round these camps—and then," Mrs. Bogart rose from her pitifulness, recovered her pace, "then I go and bring into my own house a woman that's worse, when all's said and done, than any bad woman he could have met. You say this Mullins woman is too young and inexperienced to corrupt Cy. Well then, she's too young and inexperienced to teach him, too, one or t'other, you can't have your cake and eat it! So it don't make no difference which reason they fire her for, and that's practically almost what I said to the school-board."

"Have you been telling this story to the members of the school-board?"

"I certainly have! Every one of 'em! And their wives I says to them, ' 'Tain't my affair to decide what you should or should not do with your teachers,' I says, 'and I ain't presuming to dictate in any way, shape, manner, or form. I just want to know,' I says, 'whether you're going to go on record as keeping here in our schools, among a lot of innocent boys and girls, a woman that drinks, smokes, curses, uses bad language, and does such dreadful things as I wouldn't lay tongue to but you know what I mean,' I says, 'and if so, I'll just see to it that the town learns about it.' And that's what I told Professor Mott, too, being superintendent—and he's a righteous man, not going autoing on the Sabbath like the school-board members. And the professor as much as admitted he was suspicious of the Mullins woman himself."

Kennicott was less shocked and much less frightened than Carol, and more articulate in his description of Mrs. Bogart, when she had gone.

Maud Dyer telephoned to Carol and, after a rather improbable question about cooking lima beans with bacon, demanded, "Have you heard the scandal about this Miss Mullins and Cy Bogart?"

"I'm sure it's a lie."

"Oh, probably is." Maud's manner indicated that the falsity of the story was an insignificant flaw in its general delightfulness.

Carol crept to her room, sat with hands curled tight together as she listened to a plague of voices. She could hear the town yelping with it, every soul of them, gleeful at new details, panting to win importance by having details of their own to add. How well they would make up for what they had been afraid to do by imagining it in another! They who had not been entirely afraid (but merely careful and sneaky), all the barber-shop roués and millinery-parlor mondaines, how archly they were giggling (this second—she could hear them at it); with what self-commendation they were cackling their suavest wit: "You can't tell *me* she ain't a gay bird; I'm wise!"

And not one man in town to carry out their pioneer tradition of superb and contemptuous cursing, not one to verify the myth that their "rough chivalry" and "rugged virtues" were more generous than the petty scandal-picking of older lands, not one dramatic frontiersman to thunder, with fantastic and fictional oaths, "What are you hinting at? What are you snickering at? What facts have you? What are these unheard-of sins you condemn so much—and like so well?"

No one to say it. Not Kennicott nor Guy Pollock nor Champ Perry.

Erik? Possibly. He would sputter uneasy protest.

She suddenly wondered what subterranean connection her interest in Erik had with this affair. Wasn't it because they had been prevented by her caste from bounding on her own trail that they were howling at Fern?

John Dos Passos (1896–   )

MANHATTAN TRANSFER

John Dos Passos graduated from Harvard University in 1916, and served as an ambulance driver and a medical corpsman during World War I. His first significant work, *Three Soldiers,* was published in 1921. Attracted to the less fortunate and a campaigner against injustices, his writings in the 1920's were a passionate indictment of American society. The passage included here, from *Manhattan Transfer* (1925), demonstrates his concern for the individuality of man.

JIMMY Herf sits opposite Uncle Jeff. Each has before him on a blue plate a chop, a baked potato, a little mound of peas and a sprig of parsley.

"Well look about you Jimmy," says Uncle Jeff. Bright topstory light brims the walnutpaneled diningroom, glints twistedly on silver knives and forks, gold teeth, watch-chains, scarfpins, is swallowed up in the darkness of broadcloth and tweed, shines roundly on polished plates and bald heads and covers of dishes. "Well what do you think of it?" asks Uncle Jeff burying his thumbs in the pockets of his fuzzy buff vest.

"It's a fine club all right," says Jimmy.

"The wealthiest and the most successful men in the country eat lunch up here. Look at the round table in the corner. That's the Gausenheimers' table. Just to the left." . . . Uncle Jeff leans forward lowering his voice, "the man with the powerful jaw is J. Wilder Laporte." Jimmy cuts into his muttonchop without answering. "Well Jimmy, you probably know why I brought you down here . . . I want to talk to you. Now that your poor mother has . . . has been taken, Emily and I are your guardians in the eyes of the law and the executors of poor Lily's will. . . . I want to explain to you just how things stand." Jimmy puts down his knife and fork and sits staring at his uncle, clutching the arms of his chair with cold hands, watching the jowl move blue and heavy above the ruby stickpin in the wide satin cravat. "You are sixteen now aren't you Jimmy?"

"Yes sir."

"Well it's this way. . . . When your mother's estate is all settled up you'll find yourself in the possession of approximately fifty-five hundred dollars. Luckily you are a bright fellow and will be ready for college early. Now, properly husbanded that sum ought to see you through Columbia, since you insist on going to Columbia. . . . I myself, and I'm sure your Aunt Emily feels the same way about it, would much rather see you go to Yale or Princeton. . . . You are a very lucky fellow in my estimation. At your age I was sweeping out an office in Fredericksburg and earning fifteen dollars a month. Now what I wanted to say was this . . . I have not noticed that you felt sufficient responsibility about moneymatters . . . er . . . sufficient enthusiasm about earning your living, making good in a man's world. Look around you. . . . Thrift and enthusiasm has made these men what they are. It's made me, put me in the position to offer you the comfortable home, the cultured surroundings that I do offer you. . . . I realize that your education has been a little peculiar, that poor Lily did not have quite the same ideas that we have on many subjects, but the really formative period of your life is beginning. Now's the time to take a brace and lay the foundations of your future career. . . . What I advise is that you follow

James's example and work your way up through the firm. . . . From now on you are both sons of mine. . . . It will mean hard work but it'll eventually offer a very substantial opening. And don't forget this, if a man's a success in New York, he's a success!" Jimmy sits watching his uncle's broad serious mouth forming words, without tasting the juicy mutton of the chop he is eating. "Well what are you going to make of yourself?" Uncle Jeff leaned towards him across the table with bulging gray eyes.

Jimmy chokes on a piece of bread, blushes, at last stammers weakly, "Whatever you say Uncle Jeff."

"Does that mean you'll go to work for a month this summer in my office? Get a taste of how it feels to make a living, like a man in a man's world, get an idea of how the business is run?" Jimmy nods his head. "Well I think you've come to a very sensible decision," booms Uncle Jeff leaning back in his chair so that the light strikes across the wave of his steelgray hair. "By the way what'll you have for dessert? . . . Years from now Jimmy, when you are a successful man with a business of your own we'll remember this talk. It's the beginning of your career."

The hatcheck girl smiles from under the disdainful pile of her billowy blond hair when she hands Jimmy his hat that looks squashed flat and soiled and limp among the big-bellied derbies and the fedoras and the majestic panamas hanging on the pegs. His stomach turns a somersault with the drop of the elevator. He steps out into the crowded marble hall. For a moment not knowing which way to go, he stands back against the wall with his hands in his pockets, watching people elbow their way through the perpetually revolving doors; softcheeked girls chewing gum, hatchetfaced girls with bangs, creamfaced boys his own age, young toughs with their hats on one side, sweatyfaced messengers, crisscross glances, sauntering hips, red jowls masticating cigars, sallow concave faces, flat bodies of young men and women, paunched bodies of elderly men, all elbowing, shoving, shuffling, fed in two endless tapes through the revolving doors out into Broadway, in off Broadway. Jimmy fed in a tape in and out the revolving doors, noon and night and morning, the revolving doors grinding out his years like sausage meat. All of a sudden his muscles stiffen. Uncle Jeff and his office can go plumb to hell. The words are so loud inside him he glances to one side and the other to see if anyone heard him say them.

They can all go plumb to hell. He squares his shoulders and shoves his way to the revolving doors. His heel comes down on a foot. "For crissake look where yer steppin." He's out in the street. A swirling wind down Broadway blows grit in his mouth and eyes. He walks down towards the Battery with the wind in his back. In Trinity Churchyard stenographers and officeboys are eating sandwiches among the tombs. Outlandish people cluster outside steamship lines; towhaired Norwegians, broadfaced Swedes, Polacks, swarthy stumps of men that smell of garlic from the Mediterranean, mountainous Slavs, three Chinamen, a bunch of Lascars. On the little triangle in front of the Customhouse, Jim Herf turns and stares long up the deep gash of Broadway, facing the wind squarely. Uncle Jeff and his office can go plumb to hell.

Charles A. Beard (1874–1948)

Mary R. Beard (1876–1958)

THE QUEST FOR NORMALCY

Charles and Mary Beard were both incisive and prolific writers of history. Charles Beard's radical and questioning approach to United States history was first developed in *An Economic Interpretation of the Constitution of the United States* (1913), but his most comprehensive work was *The Rise of American Civilization* (1927), co-authored with his wife. In the following excerpt from the latter book, the Beards offer several reasons for the intellectual discontent of the 1920's as it operated in politics.

IN ONLY one relation did the Wilson administration persist in exercising unsparing control over private affairs once justified by the demands of the war, namely, in the suppression of critical opinion. To the petition for a general amnesty and oblivion which circulated soon after the armistice, the President turned a face of steel. With his approval, the Postmaster General, Burleson, continued to exercise a stringent supervision over the press and the mails. With the same high benediction, the Attorney General, A. Mitchell Palmer, candidate for the Democratic nomination, kept himself in the public eye by a hot "war on the Reds," arresting suspected persons wholesale, permitting the use of provocative agents to stir up "seditious meetings," insisting on the deportation of aliens rounded up by detectives from the Department of Justice, and tolerating if not authorizing constant resort to the third degree, that is, the physical abuse of accused persons.

Indeed the inquisitorial activities of the Wilson administration after the close of the "war to make the world safe for democracy" became so vehement that a committee of prominent lawyers filed a memorandum of remonstrance. In the name of constitutional rights, Charles E. Hughes, a man given to measured language, warmly protested in an address delivered in the summer of 1920 before the Harvard law alumni, speaking with deep concern about inflammatory appeals to prejudice made by district attorneys and about the browbeating of witnesses during trial by judges in every kind of court and in every part of the country. "We may well wonder, in view of the precedents now established," exclaimed the former Justice of the Supreme Court, "whether constitutional government as heretofore maintained in this republic could survive another great war even victoriously waged." It was only by the most strenuous efforts that persons of liberal tendencies were able to prevent Congress from passing, in days of peace, a new sedition bill more drastic than the measure enacted ostensibly for martial purposes; and in spite of their efforts many war statutes affecting civil liberties were retained in force long after the close of the European conflict.

By many hands, therefore, the stage was set for a strong reaction against everything that had a Wilsonian flavor. Business men could not forgive him for the tariff act, the Adamson law fixing an eight hour day for trainmen, his Mexican policy, his indifference to many appeals for favors, and the heavy taxes laid on private and corporate incomes—to mention some of a hundred items. German-Americans were resentful because he had helped to effect the downfall of the German Empire. Irish-Americans were furious about the aid rendered to Great Britain. Liberals fumed over "his surrender to British and French imperialism at Paris," his blunt refusal to approve a general amnesty for political offenders, and his continued prosecution of persons accused of harboring radical opinions. Republican statesmen who had endured and even ostentatiously approved Wilson's lofty sentiments about the objects of the war now felt free to deny the official hypothesis, assail it violently, and substitute for it the simple and less seraphic reason that we had taken up arms "to save our skins."

In fact on all sides the canonical creed of the war, the enthralling idealism with which Wilson had sustained his grand crusade, was now attacked with relentless analysis—much to the amazement of the Socialists in jail for the objections they had so recently put on record in the court of opinion against the official hypothesis. At the origin of the conflict, the European belligerents later associated with the United States in that high enterprise had not made professions directly contrary to their real sentiments incorporated in the Secret Treaties, and in the hour of distress they had accepted Wilson's ethical flourishes merely as a garnish to the substantial aid that accompanied them. Once safely over the hazards of war and in secure possession of the fruits of a draconian peace, they indulgently allowed critical writers to turn heavy batteries upon the most elaborate of their former defense mechanisms.

With an unconcern that astounded the generality, Sir Philip Gibbs now characterized the Belgian atrocity stories as pure war myths and portrayed the Allied leaders as cynical and contemptuous gamblers in the lives of boys. Freed from official censorship this brilliant journalist, whose livid etchings of the war had thrilled millions during the tragic years and had given the Allied leaders heroic proportions, angrily dubbed the patriot statesmen of the war for democracy "the Gang." In vitriolic language, he condemned the "hard materialist outlook" of Balfour, Law, Curzon, and Carson in his own country.

Then after exclaiming contemptuously "Is there any soul in England who believes in the wisdom of Winston Churchill?" Gibbs laughed at Clemenceau, "the indomitable Tiger of French victory," declaring that "he looked more like a walrus than a tiger, a poor old walrus in a traveling circus." Having thrown Clemenceau from his pedestal, the indignant journalist paid his respects to that "peerless champion of liberty and the right," Raymond Poincaré, M. le Président de Bordeaux, "with plump waxen face, expressionless and, I thought, merely stupid." Through with them as individuals, Gibbs rendered a collective judgment: "The old politicians who had played the game of politics before the war, gambling with the lives of men for territories, privileged markets, oil fields, native races, coaling stations, and imperial prestige, grabbed the pool which the German gamblers had lost when their last bluff was called and quarrelled over its distribution."

To the confessions of once-muzzled journalists were added more impressive documents. When Russian, German, and Austrian archives were torn open by revolution, the secret negotiations, conversations, agreements, and treaties by which the Entente Powers had planned to break Germany and divide the spoils of war according to the ancient rules were exposed to the public gaze. In all its naked horror the sordid and grimy diplomacy which had precipitated the bloody conflict was revealed; and by way of supplement memoirs, papers, treatises, and articles on the background of the war began to flow from the presses. Though cautious editors long ignored the researches of scholars, though aged club men and embattled women continued to fight the war along canonical lines, the task of keeping alive the old reverie was far beyond their powers.

And after a while misgivings leaked into the very Senate of the United States. In the chamber that three short years before had carried the war resolution in a tempest of enthusiasm, the question was now calmly asked: "Why after all did we enter the war?" To most Democrats this inquiry was worse than indecent; it was profane. But Republicans pressed it and Senator Harding answered. Referring to the preamble of the measure declaring hostilities against Germany, he recited the acts of violence committed by the German government against the people of the United States. Then he closed laconically: "There is the whole story. Nothing there especially proclaiming democracy and humanity." This he said in no captious mood; at bottom it expressed his mature conviction. A little later in his speech accepting the presidential nomination, Harding took pains to state formally that "we asked the sons of this republic to defend our national rights" rather than to "purge the Old World of the accumulated ills of rivalry and greed." So the politicians seemed to blow mists of doubt athwart the sunlight that streamed down on the poppies in Flanders fields, bringing anguish to those who felt with Wilson that the heart of humanity would break if the United States did not enter the League of Nations.

Irving Babbitt (1865–1933)

DEMOCRACY AND STANDARDS

A distinguished student of French Romanticism and a respected critic, Irving Babbitt was also a humanistic philosopher. While he was often arbitrary and dogmatic, he nevertheless demonstrated a genuine concern for the quality of life in America. The selection presented here is from *Democracy and Leadership* (1924) and probes the shortcomings of American life in the 1920's.

JUDGED by any quantitative test, the American achievement is impressive. We have ninety per cent of the motors of the world and control seventy-five per cent of its oil; we produce sixty per cent of the world's steel, seventy per cent of its copper, and eighty per cent of its telephones and typewriters. This and similar statistical proof of our material preeminence, which would have made a Greek apprehensive of Nemesis, seems to inspire in many Americans an almost lyrical complacency. They are not only quantitative in their estimates of our present accomplishment, but even more so if possible in what they anticipate for the future. Now that we have fifteen million automobiles they feel, with Mr. Henry Ford, that we can have no higher ambition than to expand this number to thirty million. Our present output of fifty million tons of steel a year is, according to Mr. Schwab, a mere trifle compared with our probable output of twenty years hence. In short, an age that is already immersed in things to an unexampled degree is merely to prepare the way for an age still more material in its preoccupations and still more subservient to machinery. This, we are told, is progress. To a person with a proportionate view of life it might seem rather to be full-blown commercial insolence.

The reasons for the quantitative view of life that prevails in America are far from being purely political. This view has resulted in a large measure from the coming together of scientific discovery with the opening up of a new continent. It has been possible with the aid of science to accomplish in a hundred years what even the optimistic Thomas Jefferson thought might take a thousand. The explanation, it has been said, of much that is obscure to us in the Chinese may be summed up in the words "lack of elbow-room." We in this country, on the other hand, have received a peculiar psychic twist from the fact that we have had endless elbow-room. A chief danger both to ourselves and others is that we shall continue to have a frontier psychology long after we have ceased to have a frontier. For a frontier psychology is expansive, and expansiveness, I have tried to show, is, at least in its political manifestations, always imperialistic.

If quantitatively the American achievement is impressive, qualitatively it is somewhat less satisfying. What must one think of a country, asks one of our foreign critics, whose most popular orator is W. J. Bryan, whose favorite actor is Charlie Chaplin, whose most widely read novelist is Harold Bell Wright, whose best-known evangelist is Billy Sunday, and whose representative journalist is William Randolph Hearst? What one must evidently think of such a country, even after allowing liberally for overstatement, is that it lacks standards. Furthermore, America suffers not only from a lack of standards, but also not infrequently from a confusion or an inversion of standards. As an example of the inversion of standards we may take the bricklayer who, being able to lay two thousand bricks a day, is reduced by union rules to laying five hundred. There is confusion of standards, again, when we are so impressed by Mr. Henry Ford's abilities as organizer and master mechanic that we listen seriously to his views on money; or when, simply because Mr. Edison has shown inventive genius along certain lines, we receive him as an authority on education. One is reminded of the story of the French butcher who, having need of legal aid, finally, after looking over a number of lawyers, selected the fattest one. . . .

One is inclined, indeed, to ask, in certain moods, whether the net result of the movement that has been sweeping the Occident for several generations may not be a huge mass of standardized mediocrity; and whether in this country in particular we are not in danger of producing in the name of democracy one of the most trifling brands of the human species that the world has yet seen. To be sure, it may be urged that, though we may suffer loss of distinction as a result of the democratic drift, by way of compensation a great many average people will, in the Jeffersonian sense at least, be made "happy." If we are to judge by history, however, what supervenes upon the decline of standards and the disappearance of leaders who embody them is not some equalitarian paradise, but inferior types of leadership. We have already been reminded by certain developments in this country of Byron's definition of democracy as an "aristocracy of blackguards." At the very moment when we were most vociferous about making the world safe for democracy the citizens of New York City refused to reëlect an honest man as their mayor and put in his place a tool of Tammany, an action followed in due course by a "crime wave"; whereupon they returned the tool of Tammany by an increased majority. The industrial revolution has tended to produce everywhere great urban masses that seem to be increasingly careless of ethical standards. In the case of our American cities, the problem of securing some degree of moral cohesion is further complicated by the presence of numerous aliens of widely divergent racial stocks and cultural backgrounds.[1] In addition our pop-

[1] For example, 41 per cent of the residents of New York City are actually foreign-born; if we add those whose father or mother or both were born abroad, the more or less foreign element in its population amounts to 80 per cent.

ulation is not only about half urban, but we cannot be said, like most other countries, to have any peasantry or yeomanry. Those Americans who actually dwell in the country are more and more urban in their psychology. The whole situation is so unusual as to suggest doubts even from a purely biological point of view. "As I watch the American nation speeding gaily, with invincible optimism down the road to destruction," says Professor William McDougall, an observer of the biological type, "I seem to be contemplating the greatest tragedy in the history of mankind."

We are assured, indeed, that the highly heterogeneous elements that enter into our population will, like various instruments in an orchestra, merely result in a richer harmony; they will, one may reply, provided that, like an orchestra, they be properly led. Otherwise the outcome may be an unexampled cacophony. This question of leadership is not primarily biological, but moral. Leaders may vary in quality from the man who is so loyal to sound standards that he inspires right conduct in others by the sheer rightness of his example, to the man who stands for nothing higher than the law of cunning and the law of force, and so is, in the sense I have sought to define, imperialistic. If democracy means simply the attempt to eliminate the qualitative and selective principle in favor of some general will, based in turn on a theory of natural rights, it may prove to be only a form of the vertigo of the abyss. As I have tried to show in dealing with the influence of Rousseau on the French Revolution, it will result practically, not in equality, but in a sort of inverted aristocracy. One's choice may be, not between a democracy that is properly led and a democracy that hopes to find the equivalent of standards and leadership in the appeal to a numerical majority, that indulges in other words in a sort of quantitative impressionism, but between a democracy that is properly led and a decadent imperialism. One should, therefore, in the interests of democracy itself seek to substitute the doctrine of the right man for the doctrine of the rights of man.

John Dewey (1859–1952)

THE CRISIS IN CULTURE

One of the chief exponents of William James's pragmatic philosophy, the Vermont-born John Dewey was also well known for his work in the field of education. He believed that a new kind of social intelligence was needed to deal with the problems of an industrial order. The following essay calls for an educational system that will liberate Americans from the mental impoverishment of a materialistic civilization.

DISCUSSION of the state and prospects of American culture abounds. But "culture" is an ambiguous word. With respect to one of its meanings I see no ground for pessimism. Interest in art, science and philosophy is not on the wane; the contrary is the case. There may have been individuals superior in achievement in the past; but I do not know of any time in our history when so many persons were actively concerned, both as producers and as appreciators, with these culminating aspects of civilization. There is a more lively and more widespread interest in ideas, in critical discussion, in all that forms an intellectual life, than ever before. Anyone who can look back over a span of thirty or forty years must be conscious of the difference that a generation has produced. And the movement is going forward, not backward.

About culture in the sense of cultivation of a number of persons, a number on the increase rather than the decrease, I find no ground for any great solicitude. But "culture" has another meaning. It denotes the type of emotion and thought that is characteristic of a people and epoch as a whole, an organic intellectual and moral quality. Without raising the ambiguous question of aristocracy, one can say without fear of denial that a high degree of personal cultivation at the top of society can coexist with a low and unworthy state of culture as a pervasive manifestation of social life. The marvelous achievement of the novel, music and the drama in the Russia of the Czar's day sufficiently illustrates what is meant. Nor is preoccupation with commerce and wealth an insuperable bar to a flourishing culture. One may cite the fact that the highest phase of Dutch painting came in a time of just such expansion. And so it was with the Periclean, Augustan and Elizabethan ages. Excellence of personal cultivation has often, and perhaps usually, been coincident with the political and economic dominance of a few and with periods of material expansion.

I see no reason why we in the United States should not also have golden ages of literature and science. But we are given to looking at this and that "age" marked with great names and great productivity, while forgetting to ask about the roots of the efflorescence. Might it not be argued that the very transitoriness of the glory of these ages proves that its causes were sporadic and accidental? And in any case, a question must be raised as to the growth of native culture in our own country. The idea of democracy is doubtless as ambiguous as is that of aristocracy. But we cannot evade a basic issue. Unless an avowedly democratic people and an undeniably industrial time can achieve something more than an "age" of high personal cultivation, there is something deeply defective in its culture. Such an age would be American in a topographical sense, not in a spiritual one.

This fact gives significance to the question so often raised as to whether the material and mechanistic forces of the machine age are to crush the higher life. In one sense I find, as I have already said, no special danger. Poets, painters, novelists, dramatists, philosophers, scientists, are sure to appear and to find an appreciative audience. But the unique fact about our own civilization is that if it is to achieve and manifest a characteristic culture, it must develop, not on top of an industrial and political substructure, but out of our material civilization itself. It will come by turning a machine age into a significantly new habit of mind and sentiment, or it will not come at all. A cultivation of a class that externally adorns a material civilization will at most merely repeat the sort of thing that has transiently happened many times before.

The question, then, is not merely a quantitative one. It is not a matter of an increased number of persons who will take part in the creation and enjoyment of art and science. It is a qualitative question. Can a material, industrial civilization be converted into a distinctive agency for liberating the minds and refining the emotions of all who take part in it? The cultural question is a political and economic one before it is a definitely cultural one.

It is a commonplace that the problem of the relation of mechanistic and industrial civilization to culture is the deepest and most urgent problem of our day. If interpreters are correct in saying that "Americanization" is becoming universal, it is a problem of the world and not just of our own country—although it is first acutely experienced here. It raises issues of the widest philosophic import. The question of the relation of man and nature, of mind and matter, assumes its vital significance in this context. A "humanism" that separates man from nature will envisage a radically different solution of the industrial and economic perplexities of the age than the humanism entertained by those who find no uncrossable gulf or fixed gap. The former will inevitably look backward for direction; it will strive for a cultivated élite supported on the backs of toiling masses. The latter will have to face the question of whether work itself can become an instrument of culture and of how the masses can share freely in a life enriched in imagination and esthetic enjoyment. This task is set not because of sentimental "humanitarianism," but as the necessary conclusion of the intellectual conviction that while man belongs in nature and mind is connected with matter, humanity and its collective intelligence are the means by which nature is guided to new possibilities.

Many European critics openly judge American life from the standpoint of a dualism of the spiritual and material, and deplore the primacy of the physical as fatal to any culture. They fail to see the depth and range of our problem, which is that of making the material an active instrument in the creation of the life of ideas and art. Many American critics of the present scene are engaged in devising modes of escape. Some flee to Paris or Florence; others take fight in their imagination to India, Athens, the middle ages or the American age of Emerson, Thoreau and Melville. Flight is solution by evasion. Return to a dualism consisting of a massive substratum of the material upon which are erected spiritually ornamented façades is flatly impossible, except upon the penalty of the spiritual disenfranchisement of those permanently condemned to toil mechanically at the machine.

That the cultural problem must be reached through economic roads is testified to by our educational system. No nation has ever been so actively committed to universal schooling as are the people of the United States. But what is our system for? What ends does it serve? That it gives opportunity to many who would otherwise lack it is undeniable. It is also the agency of important welding and fusing processes. These are conditions of creation of a mind that will constitute a distinctive type of culture. But they are conditions only. If our public-school system merely turns out efficient industrial fodder and citizenship fodder in a state controlled by pecuniary industry, as other schools in other nations have turned out efficient cannon fodder, it is not helping to solve the problem of building up a distinctive American culture; it is only aggravating the problem. That which prevents the schools from doing their educational work freely is precisely the pressure—for the most part indirect, to be sure—of domination by the money-motif of our economic régime. The subject is too large to deal with here. But the distinguishing trait of the American student body in our higher schools is a kind of intellectual immaturity. This immaturity is mainly due to their enforced mental seclusion; there is, in their schooling, little free and disinterested concern with the underlying social problems of our civilization. Other typical evidence is found in the training of engineers. Thorstein Veblen—and many others have since repeated his idea—pointed out the strategic position occupied by the engineer in our industrial and technological activity. Engineering schools give excellent technical training. Where is the school that pays systematic attention to the potential social function of the engineering profession?

I refer to the schools in connection with this problem of American culture because they are the formal agencies for producing those mental attitudes, those modes of feeling and thinking, which are the essence of a distinctive culture. But they are not the ultimate formative force. Social institutions, the trend of occupations, the pattern of social arrangements, are the finally controlling influences in shaping minds. The immaturity nurtured in schools is carried over into life. If we Americans manifest, as compared with those of other countries who have had the benefits of higher schooling, a kind of infantilism, it is because our own schooling so largely evades serious consideration of the deeper issues of social life; for it is only through induction into realities that mind can be matured. Consequently the effective education, that which really leaves a stamp on character and thought, is obtained when graduates come to take their part in the activities of an adult society which put exaggerated emphasis upon business and the results of business success. Such an education is at best extremely one-sided; it operates to create the specialized "business mind," and this, in turn, is manifested in leisure as well as in business itself. The one-sidedness is accentuated because of the tragic irrelevancy of prior schooling to the controlling realities of social life. There is little preparation to induce either hardy resistance, discriminating criticism, or the vision and desire to direct economic forces in new channels.

If, then, I select education for special notice, it is because education—in the broad sense of formation of fundamental attitudes of imagination, desire and thinking—is strictly correlative with culture in its inclusive social sense. It is because the educative influence of economic and political institutions is, in the last analysis, even more important than their immediate economic consequences. The mental poverty that comes from one-sided distortion of mind is ultimately more significant than poverty in material goods. To make this assertion is not to gloss over the material harshness that exists. It is rather to point out that under present conditions these material results cannot be separated from development of mind and character. Destitution on the one side and wealth on the other are factors in the determination of that psychological and moral constitution which is the source and the measure of attained culture. I can think of nothing more childishly futile, for example, than the attempt to bring "art" and esthetic enjoyment externally to the multitudes who work in the ugliest surroundings and who leave their ugly factories only to go through depressing streets to eat, sleep and carry on their domestic occupations in grimy, sordid homes. The interest of the younger generation in art and esthetic matters is a hopeful sign of the growth of culture in its narrower sense. But it will readily turn into an escape mechanism unless it develops into an alert interest in the conditions which determine the esthetic environment of the vast multitudes who now live, work and play in surroundings that perforce degrade their tastes and that unconsciously educate them into desire for any kind of enjoyment as long as it is cheap and "exciting."

Walter Lippmann (1889–)

CALVIN COOLIDGE: PURITANISM DELUXE

Early in his journalistic career, Walter Lippmann gained a reputation as one of America's leading public philosophers. Not bound by any particular political party, and exercising an independence of judgment as dictated by his own conscience, he has been a perceptive commentator on every president since Woodrow Wilson. In this article he passes a rather harsh judgment on Calvin Coolidge and the generation responsible for his election.

MR. COOLIDGE'S genius for inactivity is developed to a very high point. It is far from being an indolent inactivity. It is a grim, determined, alert inactivity which keeps Mr. Coolidge occupied constantly. Nobody has ever worked harder at inactivity, with such force of character, with such unremitting attention to detail, with such conscientious devotion to the task. Inactivity is a political philosophy and a party program with Mr. Coolidge, and nobody should mistake his unflinching adherence to it for a soft and easy desire to let things slide. Mr. Coolidge's inactivity is not merely the absence of activity. It is on the contrary a steady application to the task of neutralizing and thwarting political activity wherever there are signs of life.

The White House is extremely sensitive to the first symptoms of any desire on the part of Congress or of the executive departments to do something, and the skill with which Mr. Coolidge can apply a wet blanket to an enthusiast is technically marvelous. There have been Presidents in our time who knew how to whip up popular enthusiasm. There has never been Mr. Coolidge's equal in the art of deflating interest. This mastery of what might be called the technique of anti-propaganda is worthy of prolonged and profound study by students of public opinion. The naïve statesmen of the pre-Coolidge era imagined that it was desirable to interest the people in their government, that public discussion was a good thing, that indignation at evil was useful. Mr. Coolidge is more sophisticated. He has discovered the value of diverting attention from the government, and with an exquisite subtlety that amounts to genius, he has used dullness and boredom as political devices.

I do not know whether Mr. Coolidge was born with this gift or whether he developed it by necessity in the absence of certain other political gifts. But I do know that in its present development it is no mean gift. The Democratic Party has good reason to know this, for the Democrats have been flabbergasted and routed by Mr. Coolidge's skill in destroying issues. The Democrats are simple folks used to heating themselves up to a terrific temperature over any issue. They only feel at peace with themselves when they are in an ecstatic broil. They simply do not know what to do with Mr. Coolidge. They hit his party an awful blow. They knocked three members out of his Cabinet and covered them with disgrace. And what happened? Did Mr. Coolidge defend his Cabinet? He did not. Did he denounce the grafters? He did not. Did he prosecute the grafters? Not very fiercely. He managed to get the public so bored that they could bear it no longer, and to make the Democrats thoroughly disliked for raising such a dull row. It was superb. To every yawp Mr. Coolidge can match a yawn. He has had the country yawning over the outcry against relieving the super-rich of taxes, yawning over Colonel Mitchell, yawning over the World Court, yawning over the coal strike. He has brought his technique to such perfection that one paper announced the conclusion of the coal strike in streamer headlines, saying "Coolidge Wins Coal Victory; Denies He Interfered."

This active inactivity suits the mood and certain of the needs of the country admirably. It suits all the business interests which want to be let alone. It suits everybody who is making money who wants to let well enough alone. And it suits all those who have become convinced that government in this country has become dangerously complicated and top-heavy, and that it is important to reduce and decentralize the Federal power. Mr. Coolidge, though a Republican, is no Hamiltonian Federalist. Mr. Slemp is right in saying that he has stopped, if not reversed, the Republican nationalizing tendency which runs from Hamilton to Roosevelt. He has just stopped it, mind you. He has not replaced it with anything. He has just stopped it while business is good.

The politicians in Washington do not like Mr. Coolidge very much, for they thrive on issues, and he destroys their business. But the people like him, not only because they like the present prosperity, and because at the moment they like political do-nothingism, but because they trust and like the plainness and nearness of Calvin Coolidge himself. This is one of the most interesting conjunctions of our age.

As a nation we have never spent so much money on luxury and pleasure as we are spending now. There has never in all history been such a widespread pursuit of expensive pleasure by a whole people. The American people can afford luxury and they are buying it furiously, largely on the instalment plan. And in the White House they have installed a frugal little man who in his personal life is the very antithesis of the flamboyant ideal that everybody is frantically pursuing. They have not only installed him in the White House, but they trust him utterly as they hear his voice on expensive radio sets; they praise him as they ride in expensive motor cars; they toast him at banquets where there is more food than can be eaten. At a time when Puritanism as a way of life is at its lowest ebb among the people, the people are delighted with a Puritan as their national symbol.

They are delighted with oil lamps in the farmhouse at Plymouth, and with fine old Colonel Coolidge and his chores and his antique grandeur. They haven't any of them the slightest intention of living in such a farmhouse if they can escape from it, or of doing the chores if they can buy a machine to do them, or of holding themselves aloof like Colonel Coolidge. But they are delighted that the President comes of such stock, and they even feel, I think, that they are stern, ascetic, and devoted to plain living because they vote for a man who is. The Coolidges are really virtuous people in the old American sense, and they have provided this generation, which is not virtuous in that sense, with an immense opportunity for vicarious virtue.

Thus we have attained a Puritanism de luxe in which it is possible to praise the classic virtues while continuing to enjoy all the modern conveniences.

H. L. Mencken (1880–1956)

THE DEMOCRATIC CITIZEN

H. L. Mencken was one of the champions of intellectual discontent, although his humorously pungent attacks on provincial America betrayed his own intolerance. The targets of his biting wit ranged from farmer to President, and from religious fundamentalism to democracy itself. The selection below displays his contempt for "The Democratic Citizen" in America.

THAT the life of man is a struggle and an agony was remarked by the sages of the remotest antiquity. The idea runs like a *Leitmotiv* through the literature of the Greeks and the Jews alike. "Vanity of vanities," saith the Preacher, "vanity of vanities; all is vanity!" "O ye deathward-going tribes of men," chants Sophocles, "what do your lives mean except that they go to nothingness?" But not placidly, not unresistingly, not without horrible groans and gurgles. Man is never honestly the fatalist, nor even the stoic. He fights his fate, often desperately. He is forever entering bold exceptions to the rulings of the bench of gods. This fighting, no doubt, makes for human progress, for it favors the strong and the brave. It also makes for beauty, for lesser men try to escape from a hopeless and intolerable world by creating a more lovely one of their own. Poetry, as everyone knows, is a means to that end —facile, and hence popular. The aim of poetry is to give a high and voluptuous plausibility to what is palpably not true. I offer the Twenty-third Psalm as an example: "The Lord is my shepherd: I shall not want." It is immensely esteemed by the inmates of almshouses, and by gentlemen waiting to be hanged. I have to limit my own reading of it, avoiding soft and yielding moods, for I too, in my way, am a gentleman waiting to be hanged, as you are.

The struggle is always the same, but in its details it differs in different ages. There was a time when it was mainly a combat between the natural instincts of the individual and his yearning to get into Heaven. That was an unhealthy time, for throttling the instincts is almost as deleterious as breathing bad air: it makes for an unpleasant clamminess. The Age of Faith, seen in retrospect, looks somehow pale and puffy: one admires its saints and anchorites without being conscious of any very active desire to shake hands with them and smell them. Today the yearning to get into Heaven is in abeyance, at least among the vast majority of humankind, and so the ancient struggle takes a new form. In the main, it is a struggle of man with society—a conflict between his desire to be respected and his impulse to follow his own bent. Society usually wins. There are, to be sure, free spirits in the world, but their freedom, in the last analysis, is not much greater than that of a canary in a cage. They may leap from perch to perch; they may bathe and guzzle at their will; they may flap their wings and sing. But they are still in the cage, and soon or late it conquers them. What was once a great itch for long flights and the open spaces is gradually converted into a fading memory and nostalgia, sometimes stimulating but more often merely blushful. The free man, made in God's image, is converted into a Freudian case.

Democracy produces swarms of such men, and their secret shames and sorrows, I believe, are largely responsible for the generally depressing tone of democratic society. Old Freud, living in a more urbane and civilized world, paid too little heed to that sort of repression. He assumed fatuously that what was repressed was always, or nearly always, something intrinsically wicked, or, at all events, anti-social—for example, the natural impulse to drag a pretty woman behind the barn, regardless of her husband's protests. But under democracy that is only half the story. The democrat with a yearning to shine before his fellows must not only repress all the common varieties of natural sin; he must also repress many of the varieties of natural decency. His impulse to tell the truth as he sees it, to speak his mind freely, to be his own man, comes into early and painful collision with the democratic dogma that such things are not nice—that the most worthy and laudable citizen is that one who is most like all the rest. In youth, as every one knows, this dogma is frequently challenged, and sometimes with great asperity, but the rebellion, taking one case with another, is not of long duration. The campus Nietzsche, at thirty, begins to feel the suction of Rotary.

But his early yearning for freedom and its natural concomitants is still not dead; it is merely imprisoned, to adopt the Freudian jargon, in the depths of his subconscious. Down there it drags out its weary and intolerable years, protesting silently but relentlessly against its durance. We know, by Freud's evidence, what the suppression of concupiscence can do to the individual—how it can shake his reason on its throne, and even give him such things as gastritis, migraine and angina pectoris. Every Sunday-school in the land is full of such wrecks; they recruit the endless brigades of wowsers. A vice-crusader is simply an unfortunate who goes about with a brothel in his own cellar; a teetotaler is one who has buried rum, but would have been safer drinking it. All this is now a commonplace of knowledge to every American school-girl. But so far no psychoanalyst has done a tome on the complexes that issue out of the moral struggles against common decency, though they are commoner under democracy than the other kind, and infinitely more ferocious. A man who has throttled a bad impulse has at least some consolation in his agonies, but a man who has throttled a good one is in a bad way indeed. Yet this great Republic swarms with such men, and their sufferings are under every eye. We have more of them, perhaps, than all the rest of Christendom, with heathendom thrown in to make it unanimous.

DEFENDERS

Mary Austin (1868–1934)

ARTIST LIFE IN THE UNITED STATES

Mary Austin did much to introduce Indian and Spanish culture into American literature. After a tour of Europe and a period of residence on the East Coast, she settled permanently in New Mexico. She published thirty-two volumes, emphasizing nature writing, poetry, fiction, and treatises. This article appeared in *The Nation* in 1925 as a reply to the question, "Can an artist exist and function freely in the United States?"

THE only consideration which justifies a reopening of the problem of artist life in the United States is the one imposed upon the artist by the success here, in so far as universal acceptance of an idea guarantees success, of the democratic idea that one person's opinion on any subject is as good as another's. That consideration is perhaps best expressed by my being asked, under conditions which would preclude my making a deeply thought and completely expressive communication upon the subject, to contribute to this symposium. For what is a symposium of this sort but the throwing of the artist's own concept of his life and its obligations to the ravening lions of unspecialized opinion? There is no subject in the world requiring so highly specialized an endowment if it is to be competently discussed, and there is no country in the world in which the artist's need for specialized criterions is so unsatisfied. This, I should say, constitutes the chief hazard of artist life in America, this constant exposure to an interested but not well-informed judgment.

Outside of this, there is no country in the world today offering the artist in any field such incomparable opportunity. The literary artist in particular finds himself almost swamped by fresh and exciting material, in constant flux and sparking with vitality. He finds in the prevailing new motor impulses, in the forming and reforming of new social patterns, and in the conflicts of racial temperaments all the possible incentives to artistic adventure, and the matrix of new forms. If he lacks the contact with great examples of art forms of the past which the European artist has access to, he has, as compensation, great natural beauty, dramatic in variety and undescribed, pouring its refreshing fountains on his soul. Nothing like this undefiled contact has happened in Europe since the glory that was Greece. There is no reason to doubt that, in spite of all the other disadvantages, work of Greek proportions will emerge from it; will eventually be recognized as having been in the process of emergence in the generation in which we now write. I have small patience with that studied belittlement of the American product which is, in part, the fretfulness of alien minds incompetent to function at the level of their opportunity, and, in other part, the product of that democratic pressure which compels the artist into a half apologetic attitude toward his own calling under the penalty, should he dare to be natural and happy and serious and exalted about it, that somebody will accuse him of thinking too well of himself. I *like* my country a lot, I especially rejoice in that section of it in which the gods have ordained me to

Mary Austin, "Artist Life in the United States," *The Nation,* CXX, No. 3110 (Feb. 11, 1925), pp. 151–152.

dwell, I am excited and hopeful in experimenting with the new forms which are arising spontaneously out of the normal rhythms of American life. But I am lonely at times for the lack of free social expression of artist joy, as well as of the normal discontent of the artist mind.

There is no use wasting any words on the fact that the great artist, whose genius is in advance of his age, has a bad time of it in the United States. He has always had a bad time of it, and probably always will. This is in the nature of human nature; no more profitable to talk about than the weather. It is possible that genius has modernly less difficulty in getting mere bread—one seldom hears now of genius actually starving to death. It is even on the cards that here in the United States we may develop some scientific way of dealing with genius that will, at least, make possible its full output, and preserve it until the generations grow into appreciation. But it is also quite certain that original and advanced genius can expect no more public appreciation now in America than it had in the days of Galileo. This being an ancient predicament of genius, it can be philosophically endured. What renders the artist life difficult to live here and now is the absence of dependable criterions either of direction or of achievement.

The sincere artist is always doubtful of his own work *after it is done*. While it is doing, he must feel sure of it; otherwise he would not be able to go on. But when the book is put forth he needs some sort of response by which he can measure his own work against other work, against impersonal standards of excellence, as these are viewed by impartial minds. For his complete expression of his potentiality he needs goals, sign posts, recognition other than his own, of his progress in authentic directions. And these, precisely, are the things which are oftenest lacking in the United States.

It is probable that the conditions which would foster high standards of criticism are lacking in democracy, and that the really great critic would find himself more at a loss here than the great artist is. At any rate the critics are lacking, or are insecurely documented. Here and there one finds men like Van Wyck Brooks or Carl Van Doren, deliberately steeping themselves in the American scene as a preliminary to pronouncing judgment on the art that it produces. But quite as often you find critics and reviewers aggrandizing their office out of their very poverty of native material to support it. Neither reviewing nor criticism is taken seriously enough to make it obligatory on the writer to treat them with uniform seriousness. So it happens that when I have written a sincere book out of mature American life, it is, as likely as not, reviewed by a young cub of twenty-three just out of college, or an equally immature Jew, born in a ghetto and raised on the East Side, who has to translate his thinking into English before putting it on paper. Not so long ago I wrote a book in which I put all that I have been able to discover about the next moment of American art, and had it disposed of by such a reviewer, in a rather important journal, with an opinion that has not been entertained by the English-speaking since the time of Chaucer, possibly not since the time of Richard the Lionhearted. And I am expected to guide my future output by things like that!

One can always get a hearing on the lecture platform, yet one has only to examine the current program of the club before which one is speaking to realize that one has not been invited to expound one's point of view but to "perform" for the entertainment of the audience and to be judged by the performance.

As for goals, there are none. There are no journals into which one is admitted only for tested merit, no prizes that are not dictated chiefly by editorial policy, and no organizations, election to which carries a cachet of excellence hard won. Unless the recently organized P. E. N. should prove to be such. As for the American Academy, its silly exclusion of women leads one instantly to suspect that a good many of the academicians might not be there if they dared to commit themselves to the standards of women writers.

The lack of these things, especially of criticism, is a serious drawback to the full and satisfying functioning of literary artistry. Nor does one quite see how in a democracy like ours, and with a mixed and unequal public like ours, these things are to be remedied. Some one with the judgment and the courage might do something by establishing awards, something like the Nobel Prize; both courage and judgment being needed to maintain adequate standards of merit against the popular notion that judgment resides in the people. Curiously, if you will question the judges of some of our popular awards, you will discover on their part a desire to satisfy the public with their choice quite as influential as the desire to make a true award. Perhaps this is one of the disadvantages of democracy which we have to take in order to enjoy its blessings. There can be no question, I think, that it pulls down the level of literary achievement perceptibly.

Personally I do not actually know that this has been the effect upon my work. For twenty-five years I have been consistently able to tell both critics and editors to look elsewhere for concessions, but I don't know whether secretly I haven't been influenced by their complete neglect of what I myself believe to be my best. Influences like this can be exceedingly subtle in their operation. What I do know is that the sense of geting no dependable help from the public spoils my temper and takes the edge off the keen joy of creation.

Theodore Dreiser (1871–1945)

AMERICA AND THE ARTIST

Theodore Dreiser began his literary career in 1892 with the Chicago *Globe*. He subsequently wrote several novels, the first of which was *Sister Carrie* (1900). By the time of the First World War he was regarded as one of America's foremost writers. In the following selection, which also appeared in *The Nation* in 1925, he discusses his attitude to his experience as an artist in America.

WITH all its defects, whatever they may be, social, religious, moral, I still cannot see that America so much more than any other country is lacking in those things which should stimulate or at least make bearable the life of an artist. I know that from the point of mental freedom it is supposed to and does present many difficulties and drawbacks—two or three million K.K.K.'s, for instance, watchful of morals, liquor, the Jew, the Catholic, the Negro; twenty or twenty-five million Catholics and Knights of Columbus, all set upon clean books, the parochial school, lower or purely sectarian and mechanical education—or none; innumerable Rotarians, Kiwanisians, Baptists, Methodists, each with a theory as to how the life of the other fellow should be regulated and what the national or State government should do to make the Ten Commandments work. And it is true that where these flourish, as they do largely outside New York and San Francisco, there is little doing intellectually or artistically.

Theodore Dreiser, "America and the Artist," *The Nation*, CXX, No. 3119 (April 15, 1925), pp. 423–425.

You can live well enough materially and socially anywhere in America if all you want to do is to talk to your next-door neighbor about his cabbages, his motor car, his radio, or how he is getting along in business. And if you are intellectually cautious, and watch your step as to what you think, you can avoid ostracism. But tread upon any of his pet theories or delusions, or upon those of the community, and then see. Yet, of course, this is old stuff critically and argumentatively among those who know. And no different, I fear, from what you would find in Russia if you failed to agree with the Communists at present; or in the back regions of France or Italy, or anywhere in India or Egypt, if you ran counter to the religious and moral notions of the middle classes. Indeed, I cannot see that at any time or in any clime or land it has been an easy matter for the artist to live and do his work. Only consider the thinker or artist under the Caliphate, under the Catholic church throughout the Middle Ages, in India under the caste system, in Russia under the czars up to Catherine, in France under the kings, in Spain, Portugal, Turkey today.

If I recall aright, Socrates with his original notions about life was scarcely *au gratin,* as we say over here, with the Athenians; and assuredly Rabelais, Molière, Shakespeare, Kit Marlowe, or—to come a little closer to our own day—Voltaire, Dean Swift, Flaubert, Anatole France, Baudelaire could scarcely be said to be *en rapport* with their time and people, or very welcome either. And one needs only recall Copernicus, Galileo, Bruno, to know that in these darling States today we are not nearly so badly off as we could be—Mr. Bryan and the cactus and jimsonweed legislatures to the contrary notwithstanding.

At first at least, and speaking solely as a humble devotee of the pen, I found America very difficult and unfriendly. The editors as well as the critics of 1900—to say nothing of the rank and file of the wide open spaces—seemed to be determined that that which smacked of continental realism or naturalism should not take root here; and for all of fifteen years I felt rather badly treated—being kicked and cuffed unmercifully. However, I did not die; and since then I have seen a change. Only think of the army of young realists now marching on New York, the scores of playwrights and critics even who vie with one another to keep the stage and the book untrammeled. Decidedly I have no complaint to make *now* and hope to have none—if only the K.K.K.'s, the hundred-percenters, and the Catholics and Methodists be quiet until I pass on.

But apart from past experiences, inimical as they were to mental freedom and artistic energy in such forms as I could master, I still found—and find yet—America as satisfactory to me, as stimulating, I am sure, as Russia ever was to Tolstoi or Dostoevski, or Germany to Goethe or Schiller, or France to Flaubert or De Maupassant. It has, or at least to my way of thinking it has, all of the social as well as the geographical and topographical variations which any artist could honestly desire. Where can you find a more cosmopolitan city than New York? And as for social, religious, moral, and political variations, pyrotechnics, idiosyncrasies, it is as colorful to me as any other land could possibly be.

But aside from that I would call attention to the fact that life is life wherever you find it—in whatever land or clime. Winds blow, storms come and go; the fortunes of men rise and fall; your worst enemy is fortuitously slain at some opportune moment or he harries you to your grave. But all in all it is *life* that the artist is facing in any land or clime—life with all its variations and difficulties, social, climatic, idiosyncratic; and these various aspects are not likely to prove colorless or without stimulus for the artist, assuming that he chances to appear. Of course I am well aware that social, or if not that then racial and climatic, difficulties or repressions are entirely capable of preventing the appearance of the artist in any form, just as climates are capable of preventing races in any form. Only consider the Middle Ages and the Caliphate. But even so. In America such conditions as are here have already been sufficient to nourish a Poe, a Whitman, a Norris, an Emerson, a Thoreau, a St.-Gaudens, an Inness; and I doubt not that within a reasonable period of time it will produce as glistening a galaxy of geniuses as any other country can boast. At least I hope so. In my particular field I see material literally for millions of novels —millions of plays. For to me every life is a book or many books or many plays. That the psychic compost of a given nationality is not such as to produce interpretations of the same in great volume is neither here nor there. Apart from Greece, England, and France, what countries have ever done so? . . .

A charge that has been (and possibly to within very recent days at least, justly) brought against America is that it lacks historic background and patina —the older lands of the world shaming it in the matter of architecture, history, art, the fanes and relics of great men and great things. Well, maybe. Yet for me at least America has always had the novelty and charm of youth, virility, ignorance, innocence, and that zest for life which is so characteristic of youth, together with all the interesting and astonishing problems inherent in its newness: exploration, government, transportation, organization. So many lacks to be supplied, so many opportunities to be seized—those of art and letters among them. And to say truthfully, apart from my own personal difficulties, I have been most heartily entertained rather than tortured by its ignorance, its gauche enthusiasm for impossible ideals of liberty, equality, fraternity, its wild dreams of its mission on this planet if not in the universe, its profound conviction (all below the thinking line, of course) that all things of real consequence in the modern world originated here. Do not the exponents of these illusions and convictions daily provide a percentage of us at least with a hearty laugh?

It may be and no doubt is a hard place at times for an intelligent man to work. There are so many strident voices—or have been in my all too brief day—bawling about the proper fields and materials with which an artist here may dare concern himself. The one hundred per cent American home, the one hundred per cent American mother and father, the one hundred per cent wife, daughter, son, the honest and God-fearing husband, brother, official, etc. And at the same time this handsome betwixt-oceans stage the scene of perhaps as ruthless and greedy and merciless a war for pelf as the earth has thus far been privileged to witness. The money barons, the trusts, the landlords, the stock jugglers, together with their handmaidens, the Comstockers, boards of moving-picture censors, busy ministers, vice-crusaders, sly agents (tools and fools) of religious and financial organizations—all so eager to compel or cajole or trick a rank and file likely at any time to become restless or contemptuous into a program of mental shoddy and soufflé such as no healthy animal nation bent upon even a semi-respectable career of constructive thought and constructive action could possibly accept and mentally live. It cannot be done, or at least I hope it cannot; yet of course that is why so many American intellectuals, to say nothing of some—a few—really important writers and artists, have heretofore gone abroad to live—James, Sargent, Whistler, Lafcadio Hearn, Bret Harte.

Essentially I know (assuming for argument's sake that tragedy is the greatest form of art) that a thoroughly prosperous country such as America is and is presumed to be might not prove creatively as stimulating as one in which misery reigns. The contrasts between poverty and wealth here have never been as sharp or as desolating as they have been in the Orient, Russia, and elsewhere; the opportunities for advancement not so vigorously throttled, and hence unrest and morbidity not so widespread and hence not so interesting. And are not "the sorrows of life the joys of art"? On the other hand, considering the individual as he must always be considered, a creature separate from his racial as well as economic environment, tragedy or the materials of art in any form are always at hand. For while a nation, of which the individual is a part, may be and often is a huge success, it does not follow that he is so. Amid the plenty of a nation the individual may well starve. Amid seemingly unbounded resources for the entertainment for the many he still may be wretchedly unhappy, alone, and devoid of that which entertains him. His temperament may be, and all too frequently is, at variance with the dreams and ideals of a thoroughly regimented mass about him. It only requires the temperament of the genius to select and portray this condition.

And obviously the artist, if he is one to arrest attention, is one with a message—some new mood, theory, or form to present, something that is new, not old, and hence of necessity at variance either with what has been said or believed or with what is currently believed and practiced. Hence all too often (invariably when the message is of any real import) he is a pariah, as much so as is the unbeliever to the Mohammedan, the atheist to the true Catholic, the theatrical producer to the Baptist; and he must shift for himself as best he may. But he is not here or anywhere long before he realizes that this is true, and in consequence seeks to make the best of an untoward scene while he does what he can.

Yet personally I must say I have found the working atmosphere far from unbearable and still so find it. (I talk of the South Seas, the Spice Islands, Egypt, China. Yet here I am and here I am likely to remain. Ah, me!) I am like the man who thinks—at times—that he hates all his relatives. He can do without them. He never wants to see them again. But every once in a while he runs into one—or one gets sick or dies and he goes calling or attends a funeral; and he finds that they aren't so completely offensive to him as he had imagined. He may not see eye to eye with them or have exactly the same tastes or wear as good or as poor clothes; but after all they are blood of his blood, flesh of his flesh, and he has all the things common to his country in common with them. They are better than aliens at that—or so he will think—tolerable, and even amusing. He may even strike up a friendship with one here and one there, or at least think kindly of them. And thus do I.

Sherwood Anderson (1876–1941)

LIVING IN AMERICA

Sherwood Anderson, born and raised in a small Ohio town, became a rebel against industrialized society and its characteristic suppression of sexual impulses and emotion. His versatility was proven when he became editor of two newspapers simultaneously, one of which was Republican and the other Democratic in sympathy. Best known for the highly influential *Winesburg, Ohio* (1919), in this particular essay he presents his opinions on the possibilities open to artists in America. This is another response to the question answered in the two previous selections.

SURVIVAL comes down, . . . to a question of nerve force. Often I have thought that the whole question of whether any American workman can go through the long apprenticeship which good craftsmanship inevitably requires—whether or not he can manage to make a living while keeping a part of his nerve force for creative work—is largely a matter of physical stamina.

Take, for example, my own case. I have published nine books and my work as a writer has received critical attention. My books do not sell in large quantities. Very well! Until two years ago I made my living by writing advertisements. Now I am trying to live by my pen and by the proceeds of a few lectures delivered during the winter months.

For many years, then, I went on writing, doing on the side other things than writing to support myself. As a young man, and before I became a writing man, I tried to build up in myself an enthusiasm for another kind, perhaps a more conventional kind, of work. I plunged into business, tried as hard as I could to make money. It wasn't in me. The effort only promised to make me a nervous wreck, and so, when I gave it up, I gave up also the notion of moneymaking. If I did not intend to give people what they thought they wanted, why should they bother about me, was what I had to ask myself.

Being naturally a rather easy-going, lazy sort of man, I quite consciously tried to build up in myself another way of life. For a number of years I had rather rushed about, my speech had become quick and sharp, and I had dived madly in and out among automobiles, rushed into offices, ridden on fast trains, and tried with all my heart and soul to make of myself a good go-getter. It wouldn't work. I really wanted to be a story-teller, a scribbler, I fancy. Then I began to write. But as a scribbler I found my days as a go-getter had set up habits in me that I were destructive to myself as a workman. How many stories I spoiled because I tried to hustle them, tried to bang them through my main force! My workmanship went to pieces —the story, the trail of which I had picked up, had not been allowed to mature in me. It was leaky, full of holes, and always for the same reason—the tale had not been felt through because I, the go-getter, had tried to hustle it.

But this hurry, this driving, rushing neurotic thing that was now playing the very devil with the only work I had ever undertaken honestly or had cared anything about was in me. It had become a part of my physical life. I had made it that. Very well, I had to make a change

Sherwood Anderson, "Living in America," *The Nation*, CXX, No. 3127 (June 10, 1925), pp. 657–658.

if I could. I began. For months I worked at that job in the city of Chicago. For two or three years I really worked at nothing else. I had to go from one place to another, and I took myself in hand. Was there any reason why I had to be at the new place in five minutes rather than in fifteen?

Surely not. I made myself stroll rather than rush. The old half-slovenly drawl in my speech which I had rather liked as a boy began to come back. That helped too. How amusing! Now even in the writing of advertisements, a job I detested, I did better work; but the men by whom I was employed were annoyed. One by one they spoke to me. "Don't! Don't drawl that way! Hurry! Always try to give the impression that you are going somewhere on a very important mission," they said. My slow drawling speech also bothered. I'm afraid I did not much care.

For myself it was working out, I thought, rather well. Now I saw a thousand things in every street I had not seen when I hustled along. Hundreds of little by-plays of life I had been overlooking now popped up everywhere, along the streets, in offices, in houses. As I could not do much talking when I talked slowly I heard more talk from the lips of others. Perhaps I began to learn a little.

I was, I fancy—in the only way I knew how—repairing my shattered nerves, nerves shattered by the hurly-burly of life, by the rush of all modern American life. And as I did this, as my technique for doing it became more a part of me, I began to look about more, began really to enjoy living. My stories, I thought, got a little fuller and rounder, they had more body to them.

As for the whole question of whether or not it is possible to live the creative life in America, here and now, why not? Surely there are plenty of stories here. And if there is little good story telling it is not the fault of life. Life does not deeply change because you ride in an automobile at thirty miles an hour rather than walk at three; and if it does, and you cannot get at life from the seat of an automobile, why not get out and walk?

Life in America is, I fancy, just what life has been in every age, only perhaps more complex and difficult to get at because we story-tellers try to go so fast. And for that matter, may it not well be that the stories we try to pick up and tell are really made more dramatic and interesting by the very speeding-up process inevitable in our hurried mechanical age? At any rate, there is the situation. A thousand new sounds, sights, smells, impacts are whipping away at the nerves in every modern American center of life.

The American who tries to escape by running off to live, say in Europe, is putting himself out of it altogether. To get at the story he has got to stay where the story is. The artist cannot change life. That isn't his job. He has got to paint it, write it, sing it—and to do that he has got to be in it and a part of it, with its rhythm in his blood.

Zona Gale (1874–1938)

THE UNITED STATES AND THE ARTIST

Born a little too early to be considered "youthful" in the decade that followed World War I, Zona Gale nevertheless echoed the sentiments of the "lost generation." Although "realistic" about her society, in the manner of Sinclair Lewis and Theodore Dreiser, she was inclined to be sentimental at times. Her writing won praise for its clarity and fidelity, as evidenced by the Pulitzer Prize awarded to her in 1921 for her play *Miss Lulu Bett* (1920). The selection presented here indicates her attitude toward the United States and its artistic environment.

CAN an artist exist and function freely in the United States? I think that he can do so if he knows where and how.

Unless he falls upon a place or a period of cliques, extolling new conformities and their resulting classification, the artist leads among men the loneliest life of them all. This he must do, because his work is as solitary as being born—more so, when you come to think of it. And it is true that in whatever country he works, even in one long ridden by prejudice and standardization, his four walls and his tools are all that he needs—during his actual hours of creation; and that in the ripest nation as in the most callow, while he is at work, the artist is independent of the state. But it is when he emerges from that room and becomes again a social being that he sighs to think—if he does—of the disabilities of his country as a garden for his growth. It is then that he fears its effect—if he does fear—upon his exalted hours of creation.

A former sigh for the lack of adequate criticism he need no longer breathe. Synthetic criticism arrived among us abruptly. The last ten years, having seen the rise of the liberal weeklies and reviews, have welcomed the rise of a critical estimate as high and free for literature, including drama, as for government, including the pageant of politics. Careful criticism of music and of painting was known in the United States much earlier than was significant literary criticism. The proportion of critical work to the totality of mere review work is still approximately that of the new pyramidal architecture of Manhattan to its old expressionless acreage of brick and brown stone; but of such cardinal criticism there is a surprising weekly amount, and it is a momentous part of our new national life in art. The growth in general art criticism is provable not only in New York, Boston, and Chicago, but in the newspapers of Detroit, Cleveland, St. Louis, St. Paul, and in the fascinating bulletins of print shops, book departments, the small galleries, and non-professional dramatic groups in Minneapolis, Milwaukee, and the Far West. There are writers putting out such subtle and synthetic comment as a dozen years ago was quite unknown to us, outside the established reviews; or inside, either. To what nation shall we turn, however, for an accurate estimate of all artists; and what have even the mellow nations not done to both the little artists and the giants? . . .

I am unable to believe that the United States is flawed for the creative worker by that which may be called a Constitutional taint. In a land in which all men are created equal, there are yet many who one can be perfectly sure are wiser than oneself. The search for mental superiors to rub up against is assuredly

Zona Gale, "The United States and the Artist," *The Nation*, CXXI, No. 3130 (July 1, 1925), pp. 22–25.

rewarded, for in every town are beings ripe, wise, international in their literary and musical loves; and these, created equal though they may have been, have become undeniably and even unpatriotically more interesting and more stimulating than their fellows. I do not speak, of course, of the privileged as such, but of the great and simple. There is in the United States a growing body of those with whom Henry Adams might now adventure toward his spiritual inconclusions. It may be charged that the American scene abounds in those who are neither great nor simple; but even the English artist of humor has some uncongeniality to meet. For such a name—to improvise—as Araminta Throgmorton is not humorous in London. And once a celebrated British critic cried, apropos of free verse: "If this goes on, what is to become of the iambic pentameter?" . . .

If I were an artist I should, in the light of my experience, stay here and confidently expect to do my work. I should know that from out the decays of Italy and the fatigues of France and the deepening impassivities of Great Britain one could look and imagine no more challenging artistic adventure than waits in this land with the unimaginative name. (Perhaps our name is our only artistic handicap. Perhaps if we had to ourselves the lovely word America, or if we were called Columbia, we should already be acquiring a fragrance as of harvests.) Name or no name, I should know that if in the ancient days I had gone questing for a field I should very likely have renounced everything in exchange for the terms of our unique life. Our breathless North American industrial towns, plump suburbs, motionless farms, preoccupied mountains; our desert, either as pure color today or as seed of the cities of tomorrow; and our little towns, faintly figuring the velvet of their vast fields, white or green—these are not mere material for art. These are the stuff of the life of art. That definition is a repetend for our thinking: Art is the imaginative interpretation of the life of the people, whatever that life may be.

Art is more than this. Art seeks to interpret the human spirit, naked in the universe, itself without nationality or academy or learned society or pension or past. The chief claim to be an artist which any artist has is his incurable gift of discerning that lovely laboring progress of the spirit. If, then, an artist looks out upon that spirit hard enough, even in this land so lacking in the scrutiny, the pattern, or the label of the past, albeit not without something of the fragrance of the universal breath, it may be that he will forget the difficulties of keeping his covenant in the United States.

He will be in no illusion. He will know, sadly enough, that he has turned from the flowered debris, the resonant footsteps, the delicate somnolence, the emanations of genius and of ruin. He will be in no illusion. And when our one hundred percenters come and tell him that he has the best country on earth to write in, he will emphatically demur. He will reply that there is no best country to write in. There are only an old world and a new. You make your choice.

II. LITERARY CRITICS OF LATER GENERATIONS VIEW THE 1920'S

UNFAVORABLE

John W. Aldridge (1922–)

AFTER THE LOST GENERATION

An educator, novelist, and critic, John W. Aldridge speaks with authority on the writers of the twenties. His literary experience both in this country and abroad lends perspective to his judgment. In the two excerpts which follow, he examines the effects of the war on their life style and their sense of loss, and how these feelings led to their self-exile from America. Aldridge believes that the experience of this exile unites the postwar writers and is a universal influence on their work. He sees them as unfortunate and even pathetic victims of circumstance whose output was blighted by their experience.

DISILLUSION AND SEPARATE PEACE

Most of the writers who began moving into Montparnasse in the early Twenties had been through the war. In one capacity or another, whether with the volunteer transport units working with the French, the Red Cross ambulance sections on the Italian front, or in the various branches of the combat army after America entered the war, they had undergone the same experiences and had the similar emotional responses that were to distinguish them as a generation. They were a generation in the purest sense, perhaps, as Malcolm Cowley said, the first real one in the history of American letters, and they had chosen to be a "lost" generation, the specially damned and forsaken, lost from all others and themselves by the unique conviction of their loss, the conviction by which they lived, wrote, and perceived the life of their time.

Like most of their contemporaries who came to maturity before 1918, these young aesthetes, of whom such an amazing number were destined to make their mark in the literary world, were deeply and sentimentally affected by the patriotic slogans and catchwords that are so much the vogue of wartime. They left college and jobs to find, in what seemed a glorious adventure, escape from boredom and a cause worthy of belief. Behind them, as their transports moved out of the harbors of New York and Boston, they left conventional training in high schools and colleges, where they had been equipped with standard attitudes and prejudices. Further back still were the farmhouses and tenements where they had been born, the fields in Pennsylvania, the streets and back lots in Chicago and St. Paul where they had first played, the woods in upper Michigan, the Big Two-Hearted River, the blue Juniatas; the unreal, only truly real world of childhood from which they had escaped, been lost, to

From *After the Lost Generation: A Critical Study of Writers of Two Wars*, by John W. Aldridge, pp. 3–5, 6–17, 20–22. Reprinted by permission of the author; published by McGraw-Hill.

which they could never return. Ahead of them lay Europe with its promises of love, excitement, freedom—the Europe they knew for its women, its paintings, its books, its Paris; the Europe they knew only from novels, steamship folders, and picture postcards.

It was no accident that so many of these young men chose to volunteer with the Norton-Harjes and the other motor units then recruiting in Paris rather than go directly into a combat service. They were still tentative, uncertain about the war and their place in it. They were attracted by the romance of serving in a foreign country with a foreign army; they had made a sportsman's decision, committed themselves to hardship and danger with the recklessness of big-game hunters and with as little compulsion beyond the thrills they expected to encounter along the way. But they wanted, at the same time, to remain disinterested and aloof, they wanted to experience the excitement of death without the pain of it. They wanted above all to be free to move on whenever their jobs stopped paying off in thrills.

Fortunately their status as American gentlemen volunteers gave them exactly what they came for. As strangers among strangers they were treated with respect. They were outside the petty restrictions imposed upon the officers and men of a regular military organization, and owing to the nature of their work and a relaxed almost nonexistent discipline, they were able to mix in comparative freedom with the civilian population. They were fed, clothed, and commanded by a government to which, since it was not their own, they owed no allegiance. They were onlookers at a struggle in which, at the time, they had no personal stake. They learned the etiquette without the experience of war, the extravagance and fatalism, the worship of courage and the fear of boredom that men ordinarily learn as the price of survival; and they lost, almost by proxy, the illusions they once had had. But if the war taught them bitterness, it was a bitterness tinged with longing and detached regret, a romantic distillation of other men's despair. They were still capable of being excited by danger and the prospect of sacrificing themselves for a noble cause, stricken to exultation by the simple poignancy of death among the poppies, melted by the spectacle of love amid the ruins of a French château. They were special observers, immunized by their nationality and the good fortune of their service from all but the most picturesque aspects of the war. . . .

But if the war experience of the Harvard aesthetes and the Grenadine Guards set the emotional pattern of the Lost Generation, gave it its nerves and its capacity for excess, it remained for those other young men who served longer and more dangerously, who were forced out of their spectatorial role and into a role of active participation, to give it character and a formal philosophy. The two together—the sentimental and essentially immature longing of the observer that expended itself in bitter, riotous play and the premature disillusion of the participant who saw too much too soon—seem to me to account for the duality of so much of the literature that generation produced, its blend of tenderness and violence, innocence and numbness; its women with the shatter-proof hearts and the broken souls; its tough young men with the look of punch-drunk boxers and the fears of being left alone in the dark; all its sad and forsaken, beautiful and damned.

Perhaps in no other novel can the twin personality of lostness be so clearly seen as in Hemingway's *A Farewell to Arms*. The love story of Frederick Henry and Catherine Barkley is, in the largest sense, the story of how the Lost Generation earned its name, how the character of its loss was revealed in its philosophical outlook, and how the spectatorial attitude proved to be inadequate to cope with the real issues of the war.

Frederick Henry is an American serving with an Italian ambulance unit. As a spiritual nonparticipant, he is able to hold himself aloof from the war and its politics. Even when his job requires him to go to the battle areas and bring back the wounded, he preserves his detachment. The war is always outside, something in which "they" are engaged, never himself—"This war . . . did not have anything to do with me. It seemed no more dangerous to me . . . than war in the movies."[1] Yet the war is always there, just over the mountains, just down the road. For Frederick Henry it serves as a permanent frame in which his own private chaos is somehow mitigated. It relates to him as belief in God relates to the priest and being a good surgeon relates to Rinaldi. Without the war he would have no tangible assurance that beyond his personal identity, the self he protects so carefully from all jars and shocks, the universe did not rush in all directions, vast and purposeless.

The retreat from Caporetto may be said to divide *A Farewell to Arms* into two parts. Up to the retreat Frederick Henry's relations with the war are primarily spectatorial, but with this difference: that after nearly two years at the front the attitudes and responses of the gentleman volunteer have been raised in him to the next higher power and become formulated into a distinct philosophical code. Onto the background of incessant war he must project an artificial system of checks and balances that will serve as a discipline for himself and his environment. Within the area of his sensibility, which he keeps tightly focused so that only the essentials of experience can come through, he feels relatively secure. But the world beyond the range of his will constitutes a perpetual threat to his safety. It is peopled with strange, violent gods and governed by a primitive jungle law. Those who do not keep themselves at all times self-hypnotized and numb it kills. "It kills the very good and the very gentle and the very brave impartially. If you are none of these you can be sure it will kill you too but there will be no special hurry." His only salvation lies in the faithful performance of the little ceremonies he has invented for himself, for it is through these that he wins the favor of the gods who hold the power of life and death.

Life for him is thus a matter of continual propitiation and restraint. He is a man walking on the edge of a bottomless abyss; the slightest misstep will send him plunging to destruction. Everything he does must be done in slow motion so as not "to rush his sensations any." What cannot be broken down to simplicity under his clenched will must be cast out. Too much thinking, particularly on an abstract level, is dangerous. Abstract thoughts, like abstract words, seduce his mind away from essential experience, the true nature of things, and make him uncomfortably aware of the shadow world outside that sometimes haunts him in sleep. It is only when the weather is clear (the rain, too, is dangerous), the war is going well, and he can concern himself exclusively with his own sensations and with the objects which arouse them, that he is entirely at ease. If at one time the emotions of war had excited him, increased his appetite for life, they now constituted the whole of life and served him as a drug against the thought of his possible death.

Within the magic circle Frederick Henry has drawn around himself, love is inadmissible. Love, like the formal religion which the priest represents, requires an emotion which is basically unselfish and beyond the control of the will. While the quick oblivion of sex is desirable because it renews the body and nerves without complicating the mind, the oblivion of love is synonymous with the oblivion of sleep and death and leads to the total extinction of the personality. Love is thus improper for a man whose existence depends on preserving a tight hold over himself and the war.

But with the introduction of Catherine Barkley, this hold is loosened, and we see the beginning of a reversal which is later realized in the Isonzo bombardment and the retreat from Caporetto. Until the moment in the garden when he and Catherine are alone together for the first time, Frederick Henry has been completely absorbed in his relation to

[1] From *A Farewell to Arms* by Ernest Hemingway, published and copyright 1929, Charles Scribner's Sons, New York.

and control over the war as fact, as objective reality. From that moment on, however, the fact of love begins to dominate the fact of war; and in the bombardment during which he is wounded, love emerges as the single certainty and the war recedes into nightmare. "I tried to breathe but my breath would not come and I felt myself rush bodily out of myself and out and out and out . . . and I knew I was dead. . . . Then I floated, and instead of going on I felt myself slide back. I breathed and I was back." Where the war had once stood as an objective order upon which he could project and give meaning to his private confusion while at the same time losing nothing of himself, it was now a destructive force that threatened to rob him of himself altogether.

The retreat from Caporetto, if viewed in this sense, is an externalization of Frederick Henry's personal withdrawal from a philosophical position which is no longer tenable. As he moves back over the congested roads with his ambulances and men toward the plains of the Tagliamento, it is as if some giant spring has been released and reality has been shifted out of context. Everything is larger than life, swollen beyond the proportions of sense. The normal processes of war are in reverse, making courage insubordinate and cowardice the rule. To him the whole affair is madness. The only thing left in the world is Catherine.

If the retreat is symbolic of Frederick Henry's separate peace, his plunge into the Tagliamento to escape the *carabinieri* is, as Malcolm Cowley suggested, an act of purgation symbolizing the death of the war and the beginning of a new life of love. "You had lost your cars and your men as a floorwalker loses the stock of his department in a fire. You were out of it now. . . . You had no more obligation . . . it was not my show anymore. I was made to . . . eat and drink and sleep with Catherine." But the removal of that love to Switzerland really prepares us for another death, for suddenly all the little signs and portents that have gone unheeded until now come together to fulfill the tragic prophecy with which the book began. There have been the lost Saint Anthony, Catherine's pregnancy and fear of the rain because, she said, "sometimes I see me dead in it," the priest's disillusion, Rinaldi's imaginary syphilis. They have all, in one way or another, been hurt by the war, and it is as if they had been released from it only to die or be lost in the peace.

When Catherine Barkley dies, the collapse of all reality is complete. Frederick Henry had believed in the war, and the war had wounded him. He had then believed in love because it promised to pay back all the war had taken away. Now love was dead, as cold and lifeless as if it had never been. "But after I had got them out and shut the door and turned off the light it wasn't any good. It was like saying good-by to a statue. After a while I went out and left the hospital and walked back to the hotel in the rain."

And that, it seems to me, was the final effect of the war upon the Lost Generation, the thing that in the end made their loss more than a loss of inhibition and gave a desperate sadness to everything they did. The war wrenched them away from the land of their childhood. It carried them forward in the long process of disinheritance which began in school, when they were divested of their local customs and beliefs, and continued through their college years when they each took on the stamp of fragile aestheticism that eventually made them more at home in Gertrude Stein's salon than on Main Street. As spectators, guests of the war by courtesy of the management, they were infected with irresponsibility, thrilled at second hand by danger, held to a pitch of excitement that made their old lives seem impossibly dull and tiresome. As participants, they learned to view all life, all human emotion, in terms of war, to pursue pleasure with an intensity made greater by the constant threat of death, and to hold tight to themselves and to the concrete simplicities (until the simple and concrete seemed to be all there was, all that was worth knowing) when the world around them seemed to be breaking to pieces. If the war hurt them, as it hurt Frederick Henry, they became numb and stopped thinking and believing. It was not their war any more. If love died they stopped believing in love too and began believing in sex. If everything collapsed and they were left with nothing, that too was all right. They began believing in nothing.

EXILE

From this sense of physical isolation and spiritual emptiness, it was easy for the young men to take the next logical step—active, conscious revolt and self-exile from a country which was neither gay enough nor cultured enough to deserve their presence. The idea of exile, like the idea of the religion of art, grew out of their need to sustain the emotions which the war had aroused in them, to keep up the incessant movement, the incessant search for excitement, and to find another faith to replace the one they had lost in the war.

Conveniently, a formal philosophical structure for such ideas had been shaping itself both before and during the war years in the writings of certain prominent social-literary critics, among them H. L. Mencken and Van Wyck Brooks. For a number of years these men had been expressing grave concern for the plight of the sensitive artist in a machine-made, standardized society. It seemed to them that life in America was tawdry, cheap, colorless, and given over to the exclusive worship of wealth and machinery; that for a young writer to do his best work in such a society was impossible. In 1921, Harold Stearns's symposium, *Civilization in the United States,* gave these ideas detailed and scholarly expansion. The thirty intellectuals whom Stearns had gathered together examined in essay form as many phases of American life and came up with the same conclusions: life in America is not worth living. If the young artist is to preserve his talent, he must leave the country. He must, as Stearns urged in his own essay, go to Europe where the creative life is still possible. To show that he meant it, Stearns left for France soon after his book was delivered to the publisher, and, whether because of his example or not, hundreds of the young men followed.

The story of what happened during those years abroad has been written and rewritten many times over. The process of exile was complete. The young men came to Paris. With their wives and children, cats and typewriters, they settled in flats and studios along the Left Bank and in the Latin Quarter. They took jobs as foreign correspondents for American newspapers, sent back social gossip and racing news; wrote book reviews, magazine articles, and stories; bet on horses, gambled, borrowed, and begged; did anything to keep alive and to prolong the show. If we can believe the stories, they were drunk much of the time, traveled considerably, and had a great many love affairs. They also managed to get an impressive amount of good writing done. The early work of Hemingway, Fitzgerald, Dos Passos, Cummings, and others bears witness to the fact. Betweentimes, when they were not drinking at the cafés, partying, or making love, they talked a lot and did a certain amount of thinking. At about this time, some of them discovered Gertrude Stein, and she, in turn, discovered among them talents worthy of her guidance. It was she, perhaps more than any other, who taught them how to make the most of their "lostness," how to develop, as had Sherwood Anderson, an idiom that would be true of their time and truly their own.

Then, as the new writing began to appear, new little magazines began springing up to accommodate it. Their titles, *Broom, Transition, This Quarter, Secession,* were indicative of their editorial policies. Fresh currents of energy were breaking out everywhere, everywhere the accent was on the new and different, the departure from old forms and techniques, the rebellion. The years of European apprenticeship were paying off in a vigorous new literature, a literature written so compellingly, with such a tragic sense of loss, that it seemed to describe the predicament of a contemporary humanity. For writers like Hemingway, Dos Passos, and Cummings, the experience of their generation—the bitterness, the monumental disbelief which the war had taught—was the only tradition. They had been uprooted from the world of their childhood with its unwavering ideals and trusts and plunged into the world of Caporetto, the Western front, the "enormous rooms" of the war; and they had awakened from the war only to find themselves in another and even more fantastic world—that of Dada, surrealism, and Gertrude Stein. If they understood only the immediate present and past, if they worshiped only the gods of sex, liquor, violence, and art, it was because they had known nothing else. Life for them would forever after be perceived and lived within the frame of the war and the emotions of war.

Thus, while Mencken and Lewis were still discovering the banalities of life back home, the young men who had acted on their indictments and fled to Europe were discovering a new language which would express themselves and their own unique experience. In Gertrude Stein the demands of a persistent originality had led to greater and greater indulgence in pure technique. Hers was an art deprived of its objective basis, lost somewhere in the convolutions of its careless meaning. The search for ever-widening suggestiveness carried the older Joyce into the limbo of dream, the ultimate subjective state beyond the necessity of words. But the young Hemingway's search for the "real thing," "the exact sequence of motion and fact which made the emotion," ended in a prose that was as crystal-clear as brook water, that was written "without tricks and without cheating," with nothing that would "go bad afterwards." Hemingway in those years was the American compromise with Dada. He was everybody's example of an American who combined the best that was in America with the zeal and discipline of the French. He was coarsely, robustly healthy in the tradition of Mark Twain and Sherwood Anderson, but he was never vulgar, almost never naïve; and in his passion for exactitude, *le mot juste,* he could only be compared with Flaubert.

This is not to say that Hemingway's was the only or even the most typical new style in the exile literature. E. E. Cummings's nervous, syncopated prose in *The Enormous Room* caught as accurately the sensibility of a world stunned by a prevailing sense of defeat; but his was a less restrained, though equally self-conscious, approach. Cummings had a more acute sense of rebellion than Hemingway. He was breaking the same ground stylistically, but he was doing it with a self-conscious violence and consequently a less steady hand. The result was a prose that struck through the pretensions of the past at the same time that it parodied them, a prose that suited itself instantly to the quick-reflexed life it was describing, and that contained the stomping discords and tingling minor harmonies of an intricate jazz symphony. If it bore little resemblance to Hemingway's prose, its purpose was nonetheless the same: to express the truth of the thing as it was at the moment it occurred, the truth stripped down to such an ultimate nakedness that, as Hemingway put it, it would be "as valid in a year or ten years or, with luck and if you stated it purely enough, always." Both men succeeded so well in conveying this exact truth, the precise emotions of despair and loss as they had known them, that these emotions were given a special currency and validity and seemed to explain the entire generation to itself and the world. Gertrude Stein had given the key to Hemingway when she had said, "You are all a lost generation," and Hemingway had written a novel around it. Now her words became the slogan of the new literature, and all the young men were trying to live up to them.

One could of course as easily make a god of lostness—and thus be saved—as one could be lost. One could think of it as an intellectual fashion rather than a condition of life and adopt its values in place of having no values at all. Besides, if one believed in nothing one was obliged to practice the rituals of nothingness, and these were good and pleasurable. One could drink and make love all night and still be holy. Yes, and if one carried it far enough, one could even reduce one's art to a deliberate exercise in futility. It was one of the ironies of art, as it was one of the ironies of the doctrine of loss, that beyond a certain point it merged with and became its opposite: the religion of art became irreligion and the lack of values became itself a value.

In the exile colony the process really began with Stein and Joyce when they renounced their native traditions and took on the traditions of pure art. It began, in other words, as it began for Hemingway and Cummings, with a search for absolutes; but it carried beyond them, and in the work of other, less dedicated writers it was turned into a process of general rebellion and misdirected defiance—rebellion against the ends which art was intended to serve and defiance of the public which would not understand those ends. If Stein and Joyce had been victimized by the idiot world and driven into the temple of art, then art would be devoted exclusively to the befuddlement of the world, and the purpose which Stein and Joyce had determined to preserve would be cast down. Art in the hands of the Dadaists was an instrument of confusion; and the obscurity which was once only the accidental by-product of an isolated, religiously fervid talent became in them the sole aim of the artist.

Dada might be said to have contained in the extremest form nearly all the attitudes on which the exile literary movement was based. If, as Malcolm Cowley has suggested, the reader of Joyce was expected to master a dozen languages, be familiar with the mythology of all races, and memorize the map of Dublin, in order to comprehend him, if the reader of Stein was helpless without her personal key to understanding, the reader of a Dada poem or novel could not hope, either through learning or a lifelong acquaintanceship with the author, to unravel a meaning. Dada, according to its adherents, had no meaning. It was dedicated to "pure" and "absolute" art. "Art," the Dada Manifesto read, "is a private matter; the artist does it for himself; any work of art that can be understood is the product of a journalist."

Dada was thus the extreme of individualism. It coupled an open rejection of audience with the belief that all communication between men was impossible. But perhaps in no other respect was Dada more typical of the tendencies of exile than in an active defiance of the world. Defiance, contemptuous rebellion, had been the motive power behind the entire expatriate movement as it had been the first principle of the religion of art. A generation of priests had defied the old commandments: a generation of Stephen Dedaluses had borne their chalices "safely through a throng of foes." But where the defiance of the chosen had led to flight, the defiance of Dada led to open war. The world, said Dada, "left in the hands of bandits, is in a state of madness, aggressive and complete madness." . . . "Let each man cry: there is a great labor of destruction and negation to perform. We must sweep and clean." . . . "What there is within us of the divine is the awakening of anti-human action." The duty of the artist was clear: he must expend upon the world the full measure of his contempt, and he must "protest with all the fists of his being" all assertions of humanity and life. And what of his duty to his art? Art was the weapon of his disgust. Its needs were always subordinate to the destructive function it was set to perform. Art, therefore, was anti-art, dedicated to its own eventual suicide. . . .

With the end of the roaring business boom of the Twenties came the end of the roaring exile of the artists. The small private incomes from securities, the monthly checks from the folks, the publisher's advances toward the writing of the next book, were abruptly sliced in half; then gradually they stopped coming altogether. Job contracts ran out and somehow failed to be renewed. For the first time the young men, and with them the actors, escape artists, clowns, and special guests who had come along to watch the fun and whose sole function was to be slightly amused were faced with the choice of stopping the show or starving. Actually there was no choice: it had already been made for them. They began quietly packing their bags and drifting toward Marseilles and Cherbourg.

A few chose to remain, the ones whose investments in Paradise had grown too large to abandon. Harold Stearns stuck it out and was making the rounds of the cafés in search of his missing friend years after the friends had gone home. He took to wearing borrowed clothes and making bad bets on the horses. He became ill and for long periods was painfully and lonesomely blind. His story in his autobiography, *A Street I Know*, is the story of the end of an era and of one man's realization too late of his own folly. When compared with his bitter indictment of America in *Civilization in the United States* it becomes sad, embarrassing reading. Our wishes that a better, more dignified end might have come to a man who felt so deeply and who wrote so well, and to a time that promised so much, gave only a little less than it promised, and made so much difference in our lives.

Yet it would be a mistake to assume that the expatriate movement died solely because of the collapse of the economic system on which it was based. It died as well from mass "over-extension of the flank," from drawing too long on resources which it did not possess. There had been signs as far back as 1927 when French workers had invaded the café terraces of Montparnasse to protect the Sacco and Vanzetti execution. There had been a series of suicides that year, and there were other suicides in the years that followed. "By 1927," wrote Scott Fitzgerald, "a wide-spread neurosis began to be evident, faintly signalled, like a nervous beating of the feet, by the popularity of cross-word puzzles . . . contemporaries of mine had begun to disappear into the dark maw of violence. A classmate killed his wife and himself on Long Island, another tumbled 'accidentally' from a skyscraper in Philadelphia, another purposely from a skyscraper in New York. One was killed in a speak-easy in Chicago; another was beaten to death in a speak-easy in New York and crawled home to the Princeton Club to die; still another had his skull crushed by a maniac's axe in an insane asylum where he was confined. . . ."[2] On December 10, 1929, Harry Crosby, wealthy expatriate poet and publisher, was found dead with a woman whom he had presumably loved and killed. On April 28, 1932, while his steamer was moving north through the Gulf of Mexico, Hart Crane jumped from the rail to his death.

The bankruptcy was spiritual as well as economic. The Lost Generation had learned the hard way that all roads, if they are followed far enough, lead back to zero. The religion of art, in spite of the great heritage it left behind, had led ultimately to the negation of art. The ways of adventure, dream, and calculated futility that had promised escape from middle-class mediocrity had led to fanaticism, creative impotence, and anarchy. All the extreme courses of action had been tried and found wanting. Even the exile itself which had begun as an escape from the sterility of the American wasteland and as a self-styled grace period for young American talent had ended, in far too many cases, in another and greater sterility and a blind alley for that talent. If the ideals which had motivated the Lost Generation were good for literature, if in the end they produced many good writers, they were bad for life and they produced as many broken human beings. For every Hemingway, Fitzgerald, Dos Passos, Cummings, and Joyce, there was a Harry Crosby, a Hart Crane, and a Harold Stearns. And even for Joyce there was a *Finnegans Wake* and for Fitzgerald a *Crack-Up*. In fact, the clear line of exile

[2] From *The Crack-Up* by F. Scott Fitzgerald (edited by Edmund Wilson), published and copyright, 1945, New Directions, New York.

influence runs through almost everything these men wrote; the strengths and weaknesses of the exile philosophy are in them all, and no matter how much they have tried to overcome it or how often some of them have succeeded in overcoming it, their common experience of exile and loss binds them all together and has helped to form them into the kind of writers they have become.

Van Wyck Brooks (1886–1963)

ON LITERATURE TODAY

Van Wyck Brooks acquired a reputation as one of America's most discerning literary critics. Basically conservative in nature, he was the author of a number of books and essays, among them *America's Coming of Age* (1915). Although he was critical of the shortcomings of American culture, he always believed that America offered great possibilities to writers who had the courage to pursue their artistic convictions. In this essay, he views the cynicism of the writers of the twenties as a disappointed affirmation of the ideals which they could not find in American culture. While he recognizes their disappointment, he criticizes them for an irresponsible failure to suggest ways to reinstate these ideals.

IN literary capacity, in vigour of style, in the number of our novelists, poets and critics, we are obviously in the midst of a revival; and I am only quoting foreign writers, English, Irish, French, Scandinavian, Russian, when I say that never before, outside this country, wherever books are read, have American writers been so influential. But, aside from this question of talent, there is another question, implied in my quotations from Leopardi and Ibsen. Among these brilliant writers, where does one find the "conscious guiding principle"? How far do they contribute to "regenerate the country"? Let the Russian writer Chekhov reply to these questions. "Lift the robe of our muse and you will find within an empty void." Chekhov said this fifty years ago, and perhaps it expresses your feeling about our current literature. You may agree with a further observation which I have found in Chekhov's Letters: "Let me remind you that the writers who, we say, are for all time, or are simply good, and who intoxicate us, have one common and very important characteristic. They are going towards something and are summoning you towards it, too, and you feel, not with your mind, but with your whole being, that they have some object . . . The best of them are realists and paint life as it is, but, through every line's being soaked in the consciousness of an object, you feel, besides life as it is, the life which ought to be, and that captivates you. And we? We paint life as it is, but beyond that—nothing at all. We have neither immediate nor remote aims, and in our soul there is a great empty space."

I quote this long passage because it suggests the dominant note of our epoch. We have, to be sure, many writers who do not convey this impression, writers who make us feel what ought to be and for whom life is noble and important. In Robert Frost, in Lewis Mumford, to mention two of these, one feels a joyous confidence in human nature, an abounding faith in the will, a sense of the heroic in the human adventure, good will, the leaven of existence. All good things seem possible as one reads these writers. I remember a remark of John Butler Yeats, the father of the Irish poet. Thirty years ago, in New York, I used to see him every day, and one day he spoke of an old friend of his in Dublin, a judge who had retired from the bench. When someone asked this judge what remained in his mind, what had most deeply impressed him, during his fifty years in the criminal courts, his answer was, "The goodness of human nature." The grand old Yeats, who also loved his species, quoted this with a smile of agreement, for although he did not take an easy view of life, he felt that a seasoned magistrate knew whereof he spoke. I have never forgotten this remark, and I have always felt that literature, if it is to carry out its function, must contain this germ of faith, and that the greatest literature has always done so. The writers who retain this faith are what we call idealists. Robert Frost and Lewis Mumford—let me repeat their names, and there are many others—stand in our time for this position. In them one feels the power of the healthy will. Whenever I think of them, I remember Whitman's line, "Allons, the road is before us."

This mood of health, will, courage, faith in human nature, is the dominant mood in the history of literature. It was the mood of Homer, and writers will always return to it, as water always rises to the level of its source. It is the warp of literature—the rest is the woof. But this is not the mood of the last two decades, and it seems as if these writers had lost the day, as if the poet Yeats were right in saying (although perhaps in quite a different sense),—

> The best lack all conviction, while the worst
> Are full of passionate intensity.

A mood of desperate unhappiness reigns in the world, and this is marked especially in most of the writers. Have you thought how strange it is that so much of the world swallowed Spengler whole?—and I do not deny that Spengler was a very great genius, I do not deny the reality of his intuitions. The temperamental cards of our time are all stacked in favour of despair, and a somewhat sterile despair. One error that an optimist makes destroys his whole case, while a pessimist can get away with murder. It seems as if our writers passively wallowed in misery, calling it fate; as if the most powerful writers, from James Joyce to Hemingway, from Eliot of *The Waste Land* to Eugene O'Neill and Theodore Dreiser, were bent on proving that life is a dark little pocket. Influence in literature goes with intensity. The intense minds, good or evil, are those that wield the power; and the genius that has moulded the mind of the present is almost wholly destructive; and even where, as in many cases, these writers are fighting for social justice, they still picture life as hardly worth the trouble of fighting for it. Their tone is cynical, bleak, hard-boiled, hard-bitten, and life for them is vain, dark and empty, the plaything, in Theodore Dreiser's phrase, of "idle rocking forces" or currents of material interest. What did Joyce's *Ulysses* say if not that life is a bad joke? What do our novelists say if not that nothing good exists, that only the ugly is real, the perverted, the distorted? You know the picture of life you find in the novels of William Faulkner, Dos Passos, James T. Farrell and so many others, who carry the day with their readers because they are writers of great power. They seem to delight in kicking their world to pieces, as if civilization were all a pretence and everything noble a humbug. There are teachers and psychologists who back them up. Only the other day I was reading a well-known psychologist who made two statements that he took for granted: 1, Men have always known that the romantic picture of love is false; 2, That which portrays the neurotic and defeated in human nature is closer to truth than that which pictures the aspirations of men. Love is a lie, in short, and the only realities are defeat and failure. This mood of incredulity and despair has penetrated millions of minds, and one finds it in the most unexpected places. There are people, educated people, who really think that Plutarch's heroes were humbugs, that Plutarch was pulling the wool over his readers' eyes when he pretended that heroes had ever existed. For these people, and they are many, all the closets are full of skeletons, for them even Diogenes was optimistic. What a gullible fellow Diogenes was—imagine wasting one's time, going about with a lantern, looking for an honest man, as if such a thing were to be conceived of! Not long ago I was talking with a distinguished professor about Eugene O'Neill's play *Mourning Becomes Electra*. He said that O'Neill had given the only truthful picture of New England, the New England not only of the present but of the past—that Cambridge and Concord a hundred years ago were just like this village in the play, whited sepulchres, full of dead men's bones. As for the old New England writers, who presented a different picture, they were all hypocrites and liars. So far has this iron of incredulity entered into the modern soul.

What this all means is seldom discussed in the critical writing of the present. Most of our critical writing deals with technical questions, and technical novelty, as it seems to me, is almost the only virtue it demands or praises. Not whether a writer contributes to life, but whether he excels in some new trick, is the question that is usually asked. It is their formal originality that has given prestige to writers like Joyce, Eliot and Gertrude Stein; and perhaps this is natural in an age of technics. But how can we ignore the larger questions involved in this drift of the modern mind? It seems to me it represents the "death-drive," as certain psychologists call it, the will to die that is said to exist side by side in our minds with the will to live. Defeat and unhappiness can reach a point where we accept them and embrace them and rejoice in our enervation and disintegration. And whether we rejoice in it or not, this literature is disintegrating. "All that is ugly," Nietzsche said, "weakens and afflicts man. It reminds him of deterioration, of danger and of impotence. He actually suffers loss of power by it. The effect of ugliness," Nietzsche continues, "can be measured by the dynamometer. Whenever man is depressed, he has a sense of the proximity of something ugly. His sense of power, his will to power, his courage, his pride—they decrease with the ugly, they increase with the beautiful." That is what I mean by suggesting that all these writers represent the death-drive. And if, with their technical virtues, they destroy our faith, our will to make the world worth living in, we cannot let their influence go unchallenged.

Now, I have an instinctive will to believe in writers. Deep down below the level where I agree or disagree with them, I like and respect them because they are writers. In less expansive moods, I admit that there are rattlesnake writers, rhinoceros, hyena, jackal writers. There are literary Hitlers and Mussolinis, who are as useful to the race as a large and active copperhead in August. But writers, as a class, as I have known them, are sensitive, scrupulous men, lovers of justice and full of good will for other people. They are almost all idealists by instinct. And so, when I see great numbers of writers bent, as they seem to be, on destroying life, I ask myself, What are the reasons for it? Why do they see only the ugly in life? Why are they so cynical and fatalistic? And are they to blame for this, or are we to blame—we, all of us, society, the world we live in? Creative minds, of all minds, are those that naturally love life most. Obviously, these writers have been disappointed.

It is a commonplace that all these writers have expressed the state of mind of a world between wars. Thirty years ago, when I began to write, the future was an exciting and hopeful vista. Everyone believed in evolution, as a natural social process. We took the end for granted. Mankind was marching forward, and the only questions were of ways and means. I do not need to say how far the first world-war destroyed this happy vista. The young and sensitive minds who grew up in its shadow were utterly disillusioned by what they saw. They felt they had been betrayed, and, as evil triumphed, they came to feel that nothing else was real. This was the case all over our world, and the triumph of reactionary forces, in the years that followed, has gone very far to confirm this impression. We have witnessed every day the success of the powers of evil, that have bragged and bullied their way towards the rule of the world. Everything good has been pushed to the wall, and even five years ago Bertrand Russell, speaking of England, said that no one could think of reform any longer, no one could think of anything but the approaching menace, the threat of these conquering forces that have darkened the world. If, in this respect, we are relatively fortunate, our writers have shared this world-depression; and their cynicism has other local causes. The optimistic picture of our life that prevailed in the last generation led to a reaction that was automatic. It was too good to be true; and as Howells, for instance, could not bear to look at the ugly things in life, the ugly things in life became an obsession with the novelists who followed. A similar reaction took place in the sphere of language. The obscenity and profanity of many of our writers seems to me as childish as the prudery of Howells; but Howells was prudish, and much of his generation was prudish, and this was bound to lead to what I call inverted prudery. Just so we had our "debunking" biographies, in reaction against the writers who drew the veil over the faults of their heroes; and in other ways too our civilization is reaping its whirlwinds. A few years ago, as a publishers' reader, I ran through a novel every day by some young man or woman who had grown up in the West or the South. They could not seem to forgive the towns they were born in—just to escape from these towns and tell the world how ugly, false and brutal they were seemed to be almost the motive of these writers in living. I think our generation will be remembered as the one in which everyone hated, often without visible reason, the town in which he was born. And the writers of whom I am speaking were obsessed with ugly memories, ugly as to material things and mostly as to spiritual. And I thought, Well, these towns were not founded with sensitive types in view. They were founded by aggressive men who were seeking an outlet for their primitive forces, and now the sensitive types have appeared and demanded their place in the sun, and their world is not ready to receive them. You know how Thomas Wolfe describes his country: "More land, more wooden houses, more towns, hard and raw and ugly . . . Ugly disorder and meanness." The moral of his novel is the moral of hundreds of other American novels: "The great masculine flower of gentleness, courage and honour died in a foul tangle." We are getting in this generation the reports of writers who have seen nothing else but this rawness and hardness. And we are getting also the reports of the excluded, the children of our newly arrived foreign population, many of whom have seen little else in all their lives but the slums and mean streets of monstrous cities, who have often known here little but slights and indignity. How far, for them, has America been the promised land of which we heard so much before the war?

It is the reports of all these classes that we are getting in our fiction—the excluded, the disinherited and the hypersensitive types who have grown up in our less developed regions. Worst of all, we have been getting the reports of expatriates, whose prestige of late has been immense. And when I say expatriates, I mean the word in our sense—not the sense it has come to have in connection with refugee intellectuals. The expatriates to whom I refer are those who have broken with their group-life, by choice, on grounds of taste and taste alone. The prestige of Henry James rose with that of Ezra Pound, Gertrude Stein, Eliot and various others. These writers, as writers, have great integrity, and they have made discoveries, both literary and psychological, that entitle them to much of their position; and you may say that where one lives is a purely personal question. Is it possible to lay down rules about it? Certainly many writers have lived outside their country and served their country or the world better by so doing. Ibsen lived for forty years abroad, and he said he had never seen his home so clearly as from a distance and during his absence. But I do not think this is true for Americans, perhaps because our roots are not so deep as the roots of men of older countries. When we leave our country we are apt to leave our roots behind us, and we fail to develop roots in any other country; and what this means is that we miss the deeper experiences that give us a mature point of view. Missing these experiences, we live on the surface, and, having evaded life because we cannot master it, we end by denying its importance—we end by denying the importance of all the primary things of life. You know how all these writers ridicule provinciality. But much of what they call provincial is basic in every civilization. No country could survive for six months without it. To escape from provinciality is good, provided we make distinctions; but, besides provinciality of place, there is also "time-provinciality," as Professor Whitehead calls it. This is the illusion that to be modern is worth all the other virtues; and the great effort of these writers is to represent the last minute, as if to keep up with the mode were more important than any of the great realities of life and death. They make much of technical questions because they have little to say otherwise, and they sneer at the great writers of the past, as Henry James used to say that Tolstoy was not worth reading, as Eliot prefers to Milton a dozen obscure metaphysical poets. To exalt the inferior over the great, in the name of their technical virtues, is a way of defending their own weakness; and Gertrude Stein has reduced their position to the last absurdity. In her theory of aesthetics, neither thought nor feeling matters. Nothing counts but the word-pattern, and the greatest thing in life is a nursery-jingle.

You know this is infantile, and in fact it seems to me that most of our current literature is written by adolescent minds. Mencken has remained a boy. The brag and bluster of Hemingway speak for a boy,—certainly a very gallant boy; so do Thomas Wolfe's poetic gropings; so does the cult of *Huckleberry Finn,* uniquely a book of boys, for boys, by a boy. Our novelists seldom picture developed types; and, if Eliot exalts the minor poets over the major poets, is it not because he does not feel the major emotional problems? If this is the case, what is the reason but a lack of the sort of attachments, to the family, to the soil, to public life, that develop the sense of responsibility and, with this, maturity of mind? Let me add that the writers I have mentioned have felt this problem; they have all, in one way or another, struggled with it, and that is why, among us, they are eminent writers. But even if they, the eminent, are adolescent—because of the conditions of our time—what shall we say of the rank and file, who are boys without the genius? The great cry of this age is that we should "face life"; but facing life means in many cases evading the most important elements of life. The world has seemed so difficult to writers, it has seemed so sinister and fearful, that to keep their personalities alive they have thrown the cargo over to save the ship. Their lives have been narrowed and desiccated, and they have remained emotionally shallow.

But, to return to their cynicism, does it really deny ideals? Is it not properly seen, rather, as a desperate affirmation of them? The depth of the despair of the present is the measure of its defeated expectation. It demands, it presupposes, the things it denies. Our writers like to say that "free will" is played out. They think they are determinists, but they always turn out to be fatalists, and that is quite a different matter. William James marked the distinction. "The fatalistic argument," he said, "is really no argument for simple determinism. There runs through it the sense of a force which might make things otherwise from one moment to another, if it were only strong enough to breast the tide. A person who feels the *impotence* of free effort in this way has the acutest notion of what is meant by it, and of its possible independent power. How else could he be so conscious of its absence and of that of its effects? But genuine determinism occupies a totally different ground: not the *impotence*, but the *unthinkability* of free will is what it affirms." There is the Asiatic attitude, and one could never imagine an Asiatic writing as Faulkner writes, or Dos Passos, or Dreiser, or Hemingway or any of our writers. It takes long generations of disappointment, hundreds and thousands of years of disillusion, to produce the deterministic frame of mind. The determinist is one who has never had any expectations, but our American fatalism presupposes hope. It does not argue that free will does not exist; it merely affirms that the will is not effective. It pays the highest tribute to the will, for it says that life is meaningless and empty precisely because of this negation. The only unthinkable thing, for American minds, is that the will should not exist; and that is the reason why, when it is not effective, its impotence seems to Americans so overwhelming.

So it appears that the mood of these writers is a kind of inverted idealism. Their harsh incredulity is the measure of their potential faith; and when I think of the loose talk about "high ideals" that governed the general mind when I was a boy, and that went hand in hand with so many abuses, it seems to me that this turn of thought should prove in the end beneficial, creative of all that it misses. The ideal has often been maintained by those who have denied it in their youth; and, while there are no Saint Augustines in my generation, or any John Bunyans that I know of, I think the mind of the country, as a whole, has had its adolescence in our time—old as the sections were, the South, New England. It has gone through terrible growing pains, but the nation will be, in consequence, more mature. It is a good thing, surely, that young people now are so exacting, so wary of hypocrisy and humbug. And is there not a visible reaction against the defeatist mind, and against these parasites and air-plants, who have thriven in a discouraged world, as Spanish moss thrives on decaying trees? I see on all sides a hunger for affirmations, for a world without confusion, waste or groping, a world that is full of order and purpose, and for ourselves, in America, a chance to build it. When Europe too had its chance, and Americans were hankering for Europe, William James wrote, "Europe has been made what it is by men staying in their homes and fighting stubbornly, generation after generation, for all the beauty, comfort and order they have got. We must abide and do the same." Europe still has its chance, no doubt; but Europe is reaping whirlwinds far worse than ours and has lost the charm for us that it once possessed. It has thrown us back upon ourselves, and America has risen immensely in its power to charm us. Thousands of novels, biographies and histories, published in recent years, have shown us what multifarious strivings and failures and what multifarious victories lie behind us; and young writers now are settling in the remotest regions, determined to find them interesting or make them so. You never hear now of Greenwich Village, which used to be a haven for the exiles from Alabama and Kansas, the West and the South; and the reason you never hear of it is that the exiles have gone back to Alabama and to Kansas. They are founding schools in Iowa City and writing novels about Montana, and some are poet-farmers in Vermont. They are cultivating their roots where the seeds were sown, and where they are sure to yield their flowers and fruit.

Bernard De Voto (1897–1955)

WASTE LAND

Considered liberal by some and reactionary by others, Bernard De Voto is a difficult critic to categorize. He earned his reputation as an historian of merit, winning a Pulitzer Prize in 1948 for *Across the Wide Missouri* (1947). Although he considered Mark Twain to be America's best writer, he also spoke highly of John Dos Passos and John Steinbeck. De Voto believed that the writers of the twenties misrepresented their society, perhaps deliberately, because of their conscious sense of alienation. In this excerpt, he is highly critical of their essential betrayal of the richness and variety of the American experience.

MR. LEWIS Gannett once alluded to "the hurt boy" who must be held responsible for much of Sinclair Lewis's work. Mr. Malcolm Cowley has studied the image of the young man so much more sensitive than the rude folk around him who appears so often in the fiction of the 1920's. A leading novelist of that decade, as an amusing conceit, itemized a collection of books which great writers of the past ought for our sake to have written but neglected to write. These are useful ideas but they provoke irreverence or even ribaldry. I have sometimes aspired to write a literary history of the 1920's describing the books which the decade might have produced *if*. If the lines had fallen to certain writers otherwise than they did.

What shapes might the literature of the 1920's have taken? If, instead of being reared in a nostalgia of the Stephen A. Douglas tradition, Mr. Edgar Lee Masters had been enlisted as a comer by the Republican politicians of Spoon River? If F. Scott Fitzgerald, instead of breaking a leg in a dolorous October, had been able to play on the freshman football team at Princeton? If Mr. Floyd Dell had been more adept at making small talk for the high school girls of Davenport? If a more critical public opinion had restrained Harold Stearns from writing book reviews and reconstructing society until such time as his ideas had grown adult enough to shave? If the talents of Mr. Ben Hecht had found their way not to the *Chicago Daily News* but to Batten, Barton, Durstine & Osborn? If the generic novelist of the period had first experienced sin in a hayloft instead of the books of Havelock Ellis, had grown up with more children of the village atheist and fewer members of the Epworth League, or had studied English at high school under the basketball coach instead of the generic middle-aged woman who admired the poems of Thomas Bailey Aldrich in the *Atlantic Monthly*?

Such speculations pollute the dignity of criticism, however, and it will be best to use another approach.

It would be illiberal to refuse such critics as I have been dealing with classification as imaginative writers but we must in some degree distinguish between literary thinkers and literary artists. Artists tend to lack skill at formal logic. They lack the staying power of systematic thinkers and tend to lapse from the strict construction of theses. Furthermore, their inner compulsions are more egoistic and the nature of their media requires even the most docile of them to try to work directly with experience instead of making the abstractions from it which give critical ideas their symmetry. In any period it is the critics who work out general ideas; art-

From Bernard De Voto *The Literary Fallacy;* pp. 95–106, 107–108, 111–112, 113–119, 123. Reprinted by permission of Mrs. Bernard De Voto, owner of copyright; published by Little, Brown and Company.

ists tend rather to apply them in detail than as a system. They tend to apply the end products, too, rather than the initial assumptions. We should not expect the novelists or the poets of the 1920's to conform always to the dominant critical system nor to work altogether within the literary fallacy. Nevertheless, on the whole they certainly did take instruction from the system. Between them and the material they set out to work with the literary fallacy did indeed stretch a membrane of theory, assumption, or prepossession which impaired their function. It is rather an attitude or a state of mind than the application of logical instruments, and what we find is infection or radiation rather than systematic investigation or report. I cannot take you through the literature of a decade in one lecture. I propose merely to examine the evidence of certain illustrations which seem to me to exhibit a relationship and a rough kind of harmony. They are all from the main current of the decade's literature, the official literature, the literature praised by writers themselves. They are also, whether consciously or unconsciously, within the final limitations imposed by the literary fallacy.

Sinclair Lewis will be remembered as the author of four novels, *Main Street*, *Babbitt*, *Arrowsmith*, and *Elmer Gantry*. Our purpose would permit us to approach them in a number of ways. We might say that their rationale shows a progressive shift from the ideas of Mr. Van Wyck Brooks to those of Mr. H. L. Mencken. We might say that their description of America is considerably more sociological than anything we have previously considered. We might say that although they show an energetic repudiation of American experience it is not an irreconcilable repudiation or even a fundamental one. We certainly ought to say that they have a greater gusto than any other fiction of the period. They are first-rate novels, and Mr. Lewis may well be the best novelist of the decade. But I have time only to inquire whether something which they lack may not be a common, and significant, lack in the literature of the period as a whole. I propose merely to inquire what Mr. Lewis's novels praise.

The critics have never been sure whether Mr. Lewis was trying to truly represent the life of his time or to caricature it, and it seems likely that Mr. Lewis has shared their uncertainty. Satire, however, has an important prerogative. So long as we understand what a satirist is driving at, we cannot ask him to tell the whole truth about it. The faithful representation of reality which other kinds of novelists hold to be their highest duty lays no obligation on him. But also there is a touchstone to satire: it has points of reference which make its values clear. Thus the spirited portraiture in *Main Street* withholds you from asking whether some aspects of life in Gopher Prairie may not have been distorted or ignored until you wonder what the town is being held against for reference. You discover that the reference is to certain adolescent ideas of Carol Kennicott. And suddenly it appears that the Village Virus which has poisoned America consists of the failure of small towns to support productions of the one-act plays of Eugene O'Neill, to provide candlelight at dinner, and to sanction lounging pajamas as evening wear for housewives. The superb evocation of the city of Zenith in *Babbitt* distracts one from values until one comes to consider the side of George F. Babbitt with whom Mr. Lewis finally developed a warm friendship and to consider the few inhabitants of the city who are held to be living the good life. Whereupon there appears so trivial an imagination of deep experience, so shallow and unsophisticated a conception of emotional relationships and intellectual activity, that one sees at once what has been left out of Zenith. What has been left out is human profundity, whether admirable or base.

Finally, when a novelist creates heroes he comes out into the open. Mr. Lewis's understanding is illuminated for us by *Arrowsmith*. Here he not only undertakes to make a sociologist's survey of the entire field of medicine in

America; he also undertakes to exalt the scientific ideal and to praise a way of life which he thinks of as heroic. We may dismiss the survey as within the prerogatives of satire, though Mr. Lewis's virtuosity blinds one to the ferocious injustice done to the Public Health Service, institutions like the Rockefeller Foundation, medical research in general, and the customary life of doctors. It is not that Mr. Lewis's Jacques Loeb, Professor Gottlieb, is contained altogether in a solution of romantic tears, or that his Metchnikoff, Dr. Sondelius, is a sophomore scientist seen sophomorically. It is rather that these characters show his conception of scientific inquiry to be debased. And in Martin Arrowsmith, the details of his career, his mind and thinking and emotions, his science and the larger science it is bound to, are romantic, sentimental, and above all trivial. Himself an adolescent whose experience is never mature or complex, he is portrayed in an adolescent conception of what he stands for. As a mind Martin suffers from arrested development, as a scientist he is a fool. Mr. Lewis does indeed picture certain genuine absurdities of scientific research in the book, but never the really dangerous absurdities. And the austerity, complexity, illuminations, frustrations, methods, goals, and conditions of scientific thinking never get into the book at all. The realities of science, worthy or unworthy, the great world of science in its entirety, are altogether passed by.

Is not the same true of Mr. Lewis's characters in general? Leora Arrowsmith is emotionally undeveloped. Ann Vickers is an immature mind and her emotions are childlike. Dodsworth is so simple a personality that one doubts if he could have managed a corporation. His wife Fran, who is Lewis's most developed character, is not developed past a simple statement of frigidity, a statement which does not disclose either the content or the roots of frigidity. Maturity of mind, maturity of emotion, complexity of character or experience, profundity of aspiration, despair, achievement, or failure—they are not discoverable in these books. They are not present in America so far as these books try to be an index to America. Mr. Lewis is not at ease when he is on the side of his characters, he is at ease when he is deriding them, when they are his butts. But his attack on them consists of showing that they are without complexity, sophistication, true power, or genuine depth. Select whatever you will, love, lust, family affection, courage, meditation, fantasy, childhood, religion, socialism, education, friendship, villainy, pain —and you find it shallow. The lives explored are uncomplicated, the experience revealed is mediocre.

Again there is no point in asking whether some part of this may be a defect of the novelist, for even if any be, a greater part certainly originates in the literary fallacy. In Mr. Lewis's work a sizable portion of our literature went out to answer questions whose answers it had worked out as assumptions in advance. The rationale existed beforehand as a chart, and when literature inquired what American life was like, it knew in advance that American life would turn out to be trivial, shallow, and mediocre. It is a short step from mediocrity to contemptibility. In the mood to which Mr. Lewis brought more energy, talent, enjoyment, and even affection than anyone else, novelists for a long time conceived of fiction as an exercise in expressing the contemptibility of American life. True to the pattern of fads, fiction began to develop specific types. There was the farm novel: frustration, cretinism, bastardy, and the squalor of the soul. A current folkway of writers was to seek the good life on little farms in Connecticut, whence frustrate peasants had been driven out, but the novel of farm life as unspeakably degraded moved all across our geography till the Pacific Ocean put a boundary to it. There was the novel of Prohibition, the novel of the repressed high school teacher, the novel of the American male as an unskilled lover, the novel which daringly denounced the courthouse gang —but a more studious mind than I has made a list. An admirer of this fiction, which he called the novel of protest, once set out to name its principal themes, with no apparent knowledge that he was writing humor: —

> the American passion for "bigness" and success, high pressure salesmanship, shoddy commercial products, poor housing conditions in urban areas, the narrow, lethargic, platitudinous, and often hysterical mob mind, corruption in government, labor injunctions, racketeering, standardization in education, industry, and art, the deportation of radicals, the abridgment of our constitutional liberties, the contract system of prison labor, militarism, the subsidizing of large corporations, political patronage, blue laws, nationalism, the legalized extortion of big business, sweat shops in the needle trades, racial prejudice, the stretch system in factories, inelastic marriage statutes, capital punishment, the entrance of religion into politics, imperialism, profiteering, a nation half boom and half broke, jingoism, rate inflation by public utilities, law evasions, our present jury system, election frauds, bigotry, child labor, the Ku Klux Klan, and wage slavery of every kind.

Of this sort of thing criticism has lately been saying that fiction had turned from experience to data, and that is true. But such a list merely names some of the ways in which fiction was finding the Americans mediocre or contemptible. One observes an omission: the list makes no finding that literary persons are mediocre or may be considered contemptible. However, in due time Mr. Hemingway was to close that gap.

By process of critical rationale, by dedication, by fashion, by a variety of other avenues, writers have come to occupy the site chosen for them by Mr. Brooks, for which Mr. Cabell found a suggestive name, the High Place. Biography has become a study of mediocrity and contemptibility in our past, apparently to excuse us by accusing our ancestors. Like fiction and criticism, it is a withdrawal to the High Place. Some writers, following Harold Stearns's manifesto, are making a literal withdrawal. In American society there is no joy nor light nor hope, no dignity, no worth; reality cannot be found there and art cannot live. So the Artist will seek societies where art can live, finding joy and hope and beauty, experience, deep in the grain, Paris, the French Riviera, Cornwall, the Mediterranean islands, Russia. What life in America abundantly lacks exists abundantly in such places. Thought is free there, art is the universal goal of human effort, writers are universally respected, and human life has a claim on the interest of literary men which in America it assuredly has not. But whether physical or only spiritual, the withdrawal to the High Place has become an established mode of literature and this mode dominates the literature to which the generality of writers acknowledge allegiance. The dedication of the High Place may be granted easily, but the illumination of its inhabitants seems to consist of perceiving the inferiorities of their countrymen. Few writers ever spoke of themselves in print as a superior class. The assumption is implicit in the critical rationale, but it is customary to speak not of superiority but of leadership. The superiority of the caste is the inferiority of the life withdrawn from. From the High Place, the Americans are the fall guys of the world, sometimes dangerous as a mob, less often pitiful as well-meaning boobs, but most often tawdry, yokelish, acquisitive, coarse, an undifferentiated mass preyed on by mass passions and dominated by mass fears.

Turn now to Mr. Ernest Hemingway's fiction for evidence to carry us a little farther. Here are memorable portraits of racketeers, thugs, hunters of big and small game, prizefighters, bullfighters, poolroom hangers-on, prostitutes, expatriate idlers, soldiers, a miscellany of touts, sportsmen, entertainers and the like, and some millionaires and writers of whom the principal assertion is that they are sexually impotent. Mr. Hemingway's themes are death, the fear of death, the defiance of death, and the dangers to which male potency is exposed—and it is easy to see what he praises. He praises aggressiveness, courage, male wariness, male belligerence, the instinctual life, war and fighting, sexual intercourse, and a few primary loyalties immediately associated with them. It is also easy to say what life is not, as his fiction represents life. Life, so far as it can be desired or respected, does not exist above the diaphragm. It is activated by digestion, the surge of adrenalin into the bloodstream at crises of danger or defiance, and the secretion of the testicles. His hero is a pre-Piltdown stage of man, a warily aggressive anthropoid who goes down fighting. Intellectual life does not exist even in rudimentary form, except that the contempt heaped on it grants it a kind of existence. There is no social life, there is not even a society. Pithecanthropus Erectus prowls a swamp so sown with danger that the honors, constraints, bonds, prohibitions, and decencies of men living together merely add another, extreme form of danger to it. They are weaknesses of less perfect animalities who have risen to the ethical and social development of, say, Cro-Magnon man; the superior, more primitive anthropoid merely uses them to destroy him. There is hardly even love, though Mr. Hemingway has written many love stories, one of which may well be the best of his period. Piltdown man couples with his female and the physical mating is clean, but the beauty of this function is corrupted when love tries to add spiritual associations to it. They are decadent—anything is decadent which may diminish male vigor or deflect its functioning. Life has grandeur in that it may aggressively defy violent death, and it has tragedy in that the defiance may be vain. . . .

From the beginning up to now, both implicitly and explicitly, with a vindictive belligerence, Mr. Hemingway has always attacked the life of the mind, the life of the spirit, and the shared social experience of mankind. Certainly he finds them contemptible; it is a legitimate guess that they scare him. The point is, however, that his disdain of intelligence, contempt of spirituality, praise of mindlessness, and adoration of instinct and blood-consciousness have many connections with other literary values held elsewhere in the general movement. They are related to the cult of pure esthetics, to the mystical cult of which D. H. Lawrence was the most gifted exponent in English, to the manias of doom that obsess Mr. Faulkner (who has much else in common with Mr. Hemingway), and to such clotted phobias as those that distinguish the work of Robinson Jeffers. If some areas of literature made a thesis of the inferiority of Americans, other areas exalted the thesis to make men inferior to the animals. It is a short step from thinking of the mob to thinking of the wolf pack, from the praise of instinct to war against reason, from art's vision of man as contemptible to dictatorship's vision of men as slaves. Such considerations, however, do not concern us. We have merely to repeat that Mr. Hemingway's fiction is separated from our common experience. By a different path he has come to the High Place. He is uncomfortable there for he finally comes to use the word "writer" as an epithet of contempt, as folklore has the wounded snake striking its fangs into its own body. But there he is and love, work, decency, achievement, aspiration, and defeat, as people know them who are neither writers nor bullfighters nor anthropoids, do not come within his awareness. Or, if they sometimes intrude on him, they only press the trigger of his scorn. . . .

Return to the question I asked toward the beginning of these lectures. If one who was ignorant of American life during the 1920's, say Mr. Geismar, were to consult the books of, say, Mencken, Lewis, Hemingway, Dos Passos, and Wolfe in an effort to understand it, could he trust their description? I answered no. We have come far enough to turn that answer into an inquiry.

Consider the work of Mr. Dos Passos. No insincerity can be alleged against him, no malice, no kind of irresponsibility, especially the kind which Mr. MacLeish charges against the generation. Mr. Dos Passos has an austere conception of the responsibility of a novelist. All his fiction proceeds from a vision of life in America since the turn of the twentieth century, a vision of the time and the society as a whole. It is conceived with great power. It is worked out with a technical mastery which no contemporary has excelled. It is never suffered to depart from his vision.

One might, of course, hold that this vision is sometimes mistaken. Thus the damage done to our society by his Ward Moorehouses and Charley Andersons would indeed have been insignificant if such men had been what they seem to Mr. Dos Passos—if they had been just feeble timeservers or drunken lechers, antlike creatures carried crazily on chips by a great flood. But they were able to damage our society because that is precisely what they were not. Because Ward Moorehouse had a powerful intelligence which he employed in clearly calculated operations with effectively mastered tools. Because Charley Anderson, as a class, did not spend his time in debauchery but instead with an ascetic sobriety and an undeviating single-mindedness operated a mastered technology in his own service, toward ends which he did not in the least misconceive.

Specific inaccuracies, however, are less important for our study than the enveloping conditions in which Mr. Dos Passos's characters exist. They are always held to his vision with complete fidelity. But, ferocious as the injuries inflicted on them are, they do not move us much. These half-drugged men and women marching past milestones of indignity toward graceless deaths do not engage us to share their pain. The truth is that they hardly seem to suffer pain. Nothing theoretical or ideological is missing. Art has not failed to put any of its instruments at the service of life. Nevertheless these creatures, these integrations of behavior, are removed so far from us that they seem to be seen through a reducing glass. They lack a vital quality, they seem like automatons. It is as if, shall I say, the doom they meet is merely a literary doom. . . .

We have examined a system of ideas which held that American culture was barren and American life malformed, tawdry, and venal. From this the next step, soon taken, was to find the cultural traditions actively evil and the life they expressed vile. It is easy to say that from this literature was gone a sense of the heroic in our past. It is easy to say that American literature had lost all feeling of the greatness of America, whether past or present, and of its place in the Western world and its promise to civilization. It is easy to say that belief in the future, the very feeling of hope, was gone. But to say this is superficial, for much more was gone.

Not only heroes are scarce in this literature. In books which leading writers wrote and leading critics praised, the gospel of the established church, nothing is so rare as merely decent people. Where in the literature of the 1920's is the man or woman who lived a civilized life dedicated to the mature values of civilization? Where is the man who accepts the ordinary decencies and practices them with good will, meeting with self-respect and courage the human adventure of birth, growth, education, love, parenthood, work, and death? The man who is loyal to his friends, believes in his country, is a good citizen, loves his wife, works for his family, brings up his children, and deals resolutely with the vicissitudes, strains, anxieties, failures, and partial successes that compose our common lot? In the official Scriptures that man either does not exist at all or exists as an object of derision. Mr. Dos Passos overlooks him, he is beyond the concern of Mr. Faulkner, Mr. Hemingway says that he lacks maleness, and when Mr. Lewis abandons his amiable or occasionally dangerous fools he is unable to conceive that man above the level of a high school boy.

Here criticism usually demurs. The final phase of finance capitalism, the cynicism of an inflationary boom, Prohibition, racketeering, the decay of politics, the Scopes trial, the Sacco-Vanzetti case, innumerable other data of the same kind—such evidence as this, we are told, appalled writers, who were right to dissociate themselves from it altogether. With an odd pride Mr. Edmund Wilson has remarked that this generation of writers attacked their culture more unanimously and more continuously than any other known to history. Even so, a vagrant mind wonders why orthodox dogma was unable to perceive in America any will to oppose these things except among literary folk. One goes on to point out, moreover, that not only decency and righteousness are gone from the people whom this literature exploits but, as well, the simple basis of humanity. And that, one decides, makes merely silly the distress which criticism tells us was behind the exploitation. If man is a predatory animal, then surely it is silly of writers to blame him when he acts according to his nature. The wolf may not be hated for wolfishness nor the boob for stupidity: the anger of literature would be idiotic. But the idea that writers might be idiotic is abhorrent and so, summing up, one turns from it to say instead that literature's dissociation from common experience, achieved by systematic logic, results in a fundamental judgment, and a false judgment, on the nature of man.

Permit me a digression. For some months a job that I had been assigned required me to listen to propaganda broadcasts beamed at the United States from the fascist powers. Every so often I heard a voice well known to me through a good many years, chanting in a curious parody of solemn high mass hundreds of judgments about this country and its people which the years had made even more familiar than the voice. It was Ezra Pound, saying the things he had been saying for thirty years. There was nothing novel about them. Mr. Pound, who had been one of the earliest and one of the most energetic workers in the movement I have been discussing, had himself originated some of these notions, perhaps, but the bulk of them he merely took over whole from what a generation of our literature was saying. I did not need to listen to Ezra Pound for this description of America—I could pick up books in my own library at random and find it nearly anywhere. The base culture, the inferior people, the decadent civilization, the blindness and depravity and disgusting stench of an evil nation, everything that Mr. Pound was saying about us by short wave was at hand in the works of the superior class. The United States government has now formally indicted Mr. Pound for treason. But does not his treason consist of his having had more guts than a good many of his fellow literary men? A number of writers who are on record as believing the same things when the fad was at its height are now on record as rejoicing that he has been pronounced a traitor. Some of the most enthusiastic propagandists of the current literary patriotism, yes and some writers who have somewhat more official positions, heartily believed the same things as Mr. Pound before the going got tough. But they didn't mean what they said? Then Mr. MacLeish is right and they were irresponsible. But they were deceived and have now found the light? That seems a little fragile for seers and prophets, it seems to impair the leadership of letters. But everyone has a right to be wrong? Surely, but it seems to me that Mr. Pound, who kept the courage of his convictions, has a little more dignity even under attainder.

Let us, however, turn from what I have called the official literature of the 1920's—the body of writing which was accepted by most writers as composing the movement, and which was conscious of itself as representing the age. Nothing about the period is more remarkable than the fact that second-rate writers were commonly less susceptible to the literary fallacy than their betters. But I propose to speak of certain first-rate writers who stood outside the movement.

To name only a few, when one comes to Carl Sandburg, E. A. Robinson, Willa Cather, Stephen Vincent Benét, and Robert Frost one enters a world quite different from that of the poets and novelists I have discussed and the critics who made out work-sheets for them. It is certainly not a world sugary or aseptic, washed clean of evil, or emptied of hate, injustice, cruelty, suffering, failure, or decay. No one in the generation has written with fiercer anger of the exploitation of men than Mr. Sandburg. No one in the generation has more witheringly rebuked the ebbing from our consciousness of certain elements of greatness in our tradition than Miss Cather or Mr. Benét. In Mr. Frost's poetry there is a resentment of indignities inflicted on men so fierce that compared to it Mr. Lewis's protest seems no more than a rowdy bellow and Mr. Hemingway's a rather craven sob. The difference is not that these writers fail in any way to be aware of evil or that any of them fail to understand the indecencies of life. It is only a difference of opinion —a difference of opinion about the dignity of man. That is all but it is a final difference, one that can never be resolved.

The poetry of Robert Frost affirms what the orthodox literature of the 1920's denies: that human experience has dignity. Human feeling has finality. Grief may be hopeless and rebellion may be futile but they are real and so they are tragic. Tragedy may be immitigable but it *is* tragedy. The integrity of experience is common to us all and is sacred in us all. Life *has* sanctity; whether fulfilled or unfulfilled, it *is* worthy, it *can* be trusted, it *has* a dignity that cannot be corrupted. The experience of men has a fundamental worth which neither other men, nor God, nor a hostile fate can destroy. Hold the poems to any light, look at any edge or angle of them, and they always come to the same focus. A worthless hired man comes back to an adopted home to die with people who know his worthlessness. A woman once mad washes her dishes beside Lake Willoughby in the knowledge of what made her mad and the knowledge that she will be mad again. A lover of forest orchids whom the acquisitive society has crippled signs a legal release, knowing exactly what it was that cut off his feet. In them all is an infrangible dignity. On that infrangible dignity of man Frost's poetry stands foursquare and in Frost's poetry American literature of our time makes its basic affirmation. Man is the measure of things. Man's experience is the measure of reality. Man's spirit is the measure of fate.

The literature we have glanced at lacks this basic acknowledgment of the dignity of man. That is why it is a trivial literature—why the Waste Land of Mr. Eliot and the Solutrean swamp of Mr. Hemingway are less than tragedy, smaller than tragedy. Bulls and male sharks may die in agony, and perhaps there is beauty in the moment of total aggressive force going down before superior force, but though the pain they suffer may shock our nerves we cannot possibly feel their death as tragic. The diminished marionettes of Mr. Dos Passos do not move us to either pain or protest. Conceived as aggregations of reflexes, they lack the humanity which alone gives significance to suffering or cruelty. The frustration of an animal cannot be tragic. The accusation that any man is base or has done evil means nothing at all, unless baseness and evil are defections from the spirit of man. Injustice is an empty word unless man is the measure of justice. There can be no sin unless sin robs man of a state of grace. . . .

I have remarked that for several years now literature has been confessing its errors. The confession of such an error as this is a confession of betrayal. It amounts to a confession that what truly was bankrupt was not American civilization but the literary way of thinking about it. That way of thinking, it is now quite clear—it is temporarily clear even to writers—was not competent to bring in trustworthy findings. It was not an adequate, an accurate, or a dependable instrument. It would not give results that could be used. The principal effort of literature has, by its own confession, failed. It has failed because of the insufficiency of its means. It has failed because a people, a culture, and a civilization cannot be held to literary values.

FAVORABLE

Malcolm Cowley (1898–   )

EXILE'S RETURN

Malcolm Cowley, a well-known literary editor and critic, writes from his own experience as a member of the "lost generation." He saw service in World War I and later returned to Europe as a literary expatriate during the early 1920's. In his *Exile's Return* (1934), from which this selection has been drawn, he favorably reviews the accomplishments of the postwar writers. In the "Prologue," he discusses the common experiences and feelings which brought them together and influenced their work, causing them to form a "literary generation." In the "Epilogue," he evaluates their literary aims and achievements, the influence of Europe and America on their style, and the relation of their literature to the American tradition.

PROLOGUE: THE LOST GENERATION

THIS . . . is the story to 1930 of what used to be called the lost generation of American writers. It was Gertrude Stein who first applied the phrase to them. "You are all a lost generation," she said to Ernest Hemingway, and Hemingway used the remark as an inscription for his first novel. It was a good novel and became a craze—young men tried to get as imperturbably drunk as the hero, young women of good families took a succession of lovers in the same heartbroken fashion as the heroine, they all talked like Hemingway characters and the name was fixed. I don't think there was any self-pity in it. Scott Fitzgerald sometimes pitied himself, and with reason. Hart Crane used to say that he was "caught like a rat in a trap"; but neither Crane nor Fitzgerald talked about being part of a lost generation. Most of those who used the phrase about themselves were a little younger and knew they were boasting. They were like Kipling's gentlemen rankers out on a spree and they wanted to have it understood that they truly belonged "To the legion of the lost ones, to the cohort of the damned." Later they learned to speak the phrase apologetically, as if in quotation marks, and still later it was applied to other age groups, each of which was described in turn as being the real lost generation; none genuine without the trademark. In the beginning, however, when the phrase was applied to young writers born in the years around 1900, it was as useful as any half-accurate tag could be.

It was useful to older persons because they had been looking for words to express their uneasy feeling that postwar youth—"flaming youth"—had an outlook on life that was different from their own. Now they didn't have to be uneasy; they could read about the latest affront to social standards or to literary conventions and merely say, "That's the lost generation." But the phrase was also useful to the youngsters. They had grown up and gone to college during a period of rapid change when time in itself seemed more important than the influence of class or locality. Now at last they had a slogan that proclaimed their feeling of separation from older writers and of kinship with one another. In the slogan the noun was more important than the adjective. They might or might not be lost, the future would decide that point; but they had already had the common adventures and formed the common attitude that made it possible to describe them as a generation.

In that respect, as in the attitude itself, they were different from the writers who preceded them. Sectional and local influences were relatively more important during the years before 1900. Two New England writers born fifteen or twenty years apart—Emerson and Thoreau, for example—might bear more resemblance to each other than either bore to a Virginian or a New Yorker of his own age; compare Emerson and Poe, or Thoreau and Whitman. Literature was not yet centered in New York; indeed, it had no center on this side of the ocean. There was a Knickerbocker School, there was a Concord School, there was a Charleston School; later there would be a Hoosier School, a Chicago School. Men of every age belonged to the first three and might have belonged to the others, had these not been founded at a time when writers were drifting to the metropolis.

Publishing, like finance and the theater, was becoming centralized after 1900. Regional traditions were dying out; all regions were being transformed into a great unified market for motorcars and Ivory soap and ready-to-wear clothes. The process continued during the childhood of the new generation of writers. Whether they grew up in New England, the Midwest, the Southwest or on the Pacific Coast, their environment was almost the same; it was a little different in the Old South, which had kept some of its local manners but was losing them. The childhood of these writers was less affected by geography than it was by the financial situation of their parents, yet even that was fairly uniform. A few of the writers came from wealthy families, a very few from the slums. Most of them were the children of doctors, small lawyers, prosperous farmers or struggling businessmen—of families whose incomes in those days of cheaper living were between two thousand and perhaps eight thousand dollars a year. Since their playmates were also middle-class they had the illusion of belonging to a great classless society.

All but a handful were pupils in the public schools, where they studied the same textbooks, sang the same songs and revolted rather tamely against the same restrictions. At the colleges they attended, usually some distance from their homes, they were divested of their local peculiarities, taught to speak a standardized American English and introduced to the world of international learning. Soon they would be leaving for the army in France, where they would be subjected together to a sudden diversity of emotions: boredom, fear, excitement, pride, aloofness and curiosity. During the drab peacemaking at Versailles they would suffer from the same collapse of emotions. They would go back into civilian life almost as if they were soldiers on a long furlough.

Some of them would go to Greenwich Village to begin the long adventure of the 1920s. Only long afterward could the period be described, in Scott Fitzgerald's phrase, as "the greatest, gaudiest spree in history." At first it promised to be something quite different, a period of social and moral reaction. The Prohibition Amendment had gone into effect in January 1920, strikes were being broken all over the country, and meanwhile Greenwich Village was full of plain-clothes dicks from the Vice Squad and the Bomb Squad. I remember that many young women were arrested and charged with prostitution because the dicks had seen them smoking cigarettes in the street, and I remember that innocent tea-rooms were raided because they were thought to harbor dangerous Reds. Then Harding was elected, the Red scare was forgotten and, after a sharp recession in 1921, the country started out to make money; it was the new era of installment buying and universal salesmanship. The young writers couldn't buy luxuries even on the installment plan. They didn't want to advertise or sell them or write stories in which salesmen were the romantic heroes. Feeling like aliens in the commercial world, they sailed for Europe as soon as they had money enough to pay for their steamer tickets. . . .

I am speaking of the young men and women who graduated from college, or might have graduated, between 1915, say, and 1922. They were never united into a single group or school. Instead they included several loosely defined and vaguely hostile groups, in addition to many individuals who differed with every group among their contemporaries; the fact is that all of them differed constantly with all the others. They all felt, however, a sharper sense of difference in regard to writers older than themselves who hadn't shared their adventures. It was as if the others had never undergone the same initiatory rites and had never been admitted to the same broad confraternity. In a strict sense the new writers formed what is known as a literary generation. . . .

They were not a lost generation in the sense of being unfortunate or thwarted, like the young writers of the 1890s. The truth was that they had an easy time of it, even as compared with the writers who immediately preceded them. Dreiser, Anderson, Robinson, Masters and Sandburg were all in their forties before they were able to devote most of their time to writing; Sinclair Lewis was thirty-five before he made his first success with *Main Street*. It was different with the new group of writers. Largely as a result of what the older group had accomplished, their public was ready for them and they weren't forced to waste years working in a custom house, like Robinson, or writing advertising copy, like Anderson. At the age of twenty-four Fitzgerald was earning eighteen thousand dollars a year with his stories and novels. Hemingway, Wilder, Dos Passos and Louis Bromfield were internationally known novelists before they were thirty. They had a chance which the older men lacked to develop their craftsmanship in book after book; from the very first they were professionals.

Yet in spite of their opportunities and their achievements the generation deserved for a long time the adjective that Gertrude Stein had applied to it. The reasons aren't hard to find. It was lost, first of all, because it was uprooted, schooled away and almost wrenched away from its attachment to any region or tradition. It was lost because its training had prepared it for another world than existed after the war (and because the war prepared it only for travel and excitement). It was lost because it tried to live in exile. It was lost because it accepted no older guides to conduct and because it had formed a false picture of society and the writer's place in it. The generation belonged to a period of transition from values already fixed to values that had to be created. Its members began by writing for magazines with names like *transition, Broom* (to make a clean sweep of it), *1924, This Quarter* (existing in the pure present), *S4N, Secession*. They were seceding from the old and yet could adhere to nothing new; they groped their way toward another scheme of life, as yet undefined; in the midst of their doubts and uneasy gestures of defiance they felt homesick for the certainties of childhood. It was not by accident that their early books were almost all nostalgic, full of the wish to recapture some remembered thing. In Paris or Pamplona, writing, drinking, watching bullfights or making love, they continued to desire a Kentucky hill cabin, a farmhouse in Iowa or Wisconsin, the Michigan woods, the blue Juniata, a country they had "lost, ah lost," as Thomas Wolfe kept saying; a home to which they couldn't go back.

EPILOGUE: NEW YEAR'S EVE

The exiles fled to Europe and then came back again. A decade was ending and they didn't come back to quite the same country, nor did they come back as the same men and women.

The country had changed in many ways, for better and worse, but the exiles were most impressed by the changed situation of American literature. In 1920 it had been a provincial literature, dependent on English standards even when it tried to defy them. Foreign countries regarded it as a sort of colonial currency that had to be assigned a value in pounds sterling before it could be accepted on the international exchange. By 1930 it had come to be valued for itself and studied like Spanish or German or Russian literature. There were now professors of American literature at the great European universities. American plays, lowbrow and highbrow, were being applauded in the European capitals. American books were being translated into every European language and they were being read with enthusiasm.

The exiles were still too young in 1930 to be responsible for the change; their effect on the international position of American writing would come in later years. So far as the change was produced by literary efforts, it was the work of an older generation. The literary scene had been dominated for ten years by a group of powerful writers that included Dreiser, Anderson, Mencken, Lewis, O'Neill, Willa Cather and Robert Frost. As a group they had fought against the prevailing convention of gentility or niceness and they had won the right to present each his own picture of life, in his own language. They had spoken with force enough to be heard outside their country, and one of them, Sinclair Lewis, would soon be the first American to win the Nobel Prize for literature. It would, however, be innocent to suppose that this award, with the recognition it implied for Lewis and his colleagues, was purely an honor paid to literary merit. There was also the fact that American literature had come to seem more important because America herself was more important in world affairs. In December 1930, when the Swedish Academy gave Lewis a prize that it hadn't offered to Mark Twain or Henry James, it wasn't really saying that it regarded Lewis as a greater writer; it was chiefly acknowledging that the United States was a more powerful country than it had been in 1910.

The representative quality of Lewis's work was emphasized in a welcoming address by the permanent secretary of the Swedish Academy. "Yes," he said, "Sinclair Lewis is an American. He writes the new language—American—as one of the representatives of a hundred and twenty million souls. He asks us to consider that this nation is not yet finished or melted down; that it is still in the turbulent years of adolescence. The new great American literature has started with national self-criticism. It is a sign of health."

Lewis answered as a spokesman for his generation of American writers. He attacked the genteel tradition that had prevailed in his younger days; he called the roll of his literary colleagues who might have received the prize, beginning with Dreiser and O'Neill; he complained of the artist's lot in American society and he ended by praising the writers of a younger generation—"most of them living now in Paris, most of them a little insane in the tradition of James Joyce, who, however insane they may be, have refused to be genteel and traditional and dull. I salute them," he continued, "with a joy in being not yet too far removed from their determination to give to the America that has mountains and endless prairies, enormous cities and far lost cabins, billions of money and tons of faith, to an America that is as strange as Russia and as complex as China, a literature worthy of her vastness."

Although the exiles were gratified by his praise of their work and liked his truculent generosity, they didn't agree with his statement of their aims. They had never felt the desire to give America "a literature worthy of her vastness." The phrase sounded too much like an invitation to make vast surveys of American geography and the American past. What the exiles wanted to portray was the lives and hearts of individual Americans. They thought that if they could once learn to do this task superlatively well, their work would suggest the larger picture without their making a pretentious effort to present the whole of it. They wanted their writing to be true—that was a word they used over and over—and they wanted its effect to be measured in depth, not in square miles of surface. Moreover, they had an ideal of perfection gained from their study of foreign writers and they wanted to apply the ideal at home. They didn't want to write family sagas or epics of the Northwest, huge as the Chicago Auditorium and with nothing inside but strangers seated on rows of folding chairs. They wanted to build smaller structures, each completely new but with the native quality of New England meeting houses or Pennsylvania barns, each put together with patient pride, each perfectly adapted to the life it sheltered.

The exiles had changed during their years in Europe and especially they had changed their notions of what American literature should be. They had gone abroad in almost total ignorance of everything written in this country before 1910—among the American classics they had read *Huckleberry Finn* and "The Legend of Sleepy Hollow" and perhaps *Moby Dick,* but that was about all. American literature wasn't taught in the colleges, except incidentally, and only the current American books were mentioned in literary discussions. The New England tradition had died of anemia. The few nineteenth-century authors who could be admired were French or English or Russian.

That continued to be the accepted opinion during their years in Europe. The exiles studied French authors: Flaubert, Proust and Gide, Rimbaud and Mallarmé. With more immediate interest they studied Joyce, who was in the tradition of Flaubert, and Eliot, who was in the tradition of the French Symbolist poets. They had more to learn from French than from English masters at the time, and moreover the French influence proved to be safer for young American writers because it was in a different language. If they had studied English authors they would have become at best disciples and at worst copyists. Studying French literature, on the other hand, they had the problem of reproducing its best qualities in another language, and it led them to a difficult and fruitful search for equivalents. The language in which they tried to recreate the French qualities was not literary English but colloquial American. That was among the unexpected effects of their exile: it was in Paris that some of them, notably Ernest Hemingway, worked on the problem of transforming Midwestern speech into a medium for serious fiction. Others worked on the problem of giving a legendary quality to Southern or Midwestern backgrounds. The result of all these labors was a new literature so different from its French models that when the American writers of the lost generation became popular reading in France, as they did before and after World War II, the French spoke of them as powerful, a little barbarous and completely original. The French critics had failed to recognize that these foreigners belonged in part to the tradition of Flaubert.

They had also rejoined an American tradition that was older than Flaubert and that was the most interesting effect of their years abroad. Ignorant of their own literature, starting over as it were from the beginning and using foreign models for their apprentice work, the exiles ended by producing a type of writing that was American in another fashion than anyone had expected. Although critics were slow to find parallels in the American past, it finally became evident that some qualities of the new writing had been encountered before. The careful workmanship, the calculation of effects even when the novelist seemed to be writing in a casual style, the interest in fine shades of behavior (including abnormal behavior), the hauntedness and the gift for telling a headlong story full of violent action—all these qualities had appeared many times in American literature, beginning with Charles Brockden Brown, our first serious novelist, and extending in different combinations through the work of Poe, Hawthorne, Melville, Henry James, Stephen Crane and many minor writers, so that they seemed to express a constant strain in the American character. Here was a tradition that had been broken for a time, but the new novelists had re-established it, and that was perhaps the most important result of their adventure. . . .

It was a better age for writers than I have made it seem—more serious, harder working, more soulful in its dissipations, and above all more fruitful. By choosing for emphasis some of its more picturesque episodes and characters I have given a partly distorted impression. By using books chiefly as texts I have done less than justice to many of the fine novels and poems that the age produced. It was an easy, quick, adventurous age, good to be young in; and yet on coming out of it one felt a sense of relief, as on coming out of a room too full of talk and people into the sunlight of the winter streets.

Frederick J. Hoffman (1909–1967)

SOME PERSPECTIVES ON THE 1920's

Frederick J. Hoffman was a long-time professor of English at the University of Wisconsin. In this excerpt, from his well-known work, *The Twenties: American Writing in the Postwar Decade* (1955), Hoffman discusses the personal values of the literary artists of the twenties and those of their society. These newly acquired values were the result of a widespread refusal to accept old traditions; instead, critics began to look at them in a new way and reformulate them in terms of what was needed. The chief virtue of these writers, Hoffman perceives, was an attempt to renew what seemed to be a corrupt and decaying culture. Stylistically, the result of their efforts was the development of new literary forms, which combined the old traditions together with new insights.

"SPIRITS GROWN ELIOTIC"

OF THE general images the literature of the decade impressed upon us, two are especially vivid as "classical" reminders of the time: the "pathos of the adolescent" and the "unregenerate bohemian." For the first there is the evidence of many occasions. It is contained usually in a gesture, the very vagueness of which served to thrill its readers. Undoubtedly the great early success of Fitzgerald's *This Side of Paradise* was due to its appeals to the mind of the younger generation. Its most popular gesture comes in the last two pages: Amory Blaine speaks up for the new generation, endowing it with the privileges of its immaturity. This new generation, "grown up to find all Gods dead, all wars fought, all faiths in man shaken," was to be more brilliantly and more fully characterized in other texts; but no other work was able to endow it with quite the glamour of lonely defiance to be found in the novel's last lines:

> He stretched out his arms to the crystalline, radiant sky. "I know myself," he cried, "but that is all."

Again, at the beginning of the decade, the moment of adolescent awareness was shown in Sherwood Anderson's *Winesburg, Ohio*, whose George Willard experiences for the first time "the sadness of sophistication":

With a little gasp he sees himself as merely a leaf blown by the wind through the streets of his village. He knows that in spite of all the stout talk of his fellows he must live and die in uncertainty, a thing blown by the winds, a thing destined like corn to wilt in the sun.

This shock of realization is like a birth into a new world. Cynicism has not set in, nor has a philosophy grown. The protections accorded normal experience are removed, and the young man is forced into a world he can never really understand. This insistence upon the youth of the generation, upon its perilous freedom, proved a strong incentive to those who could claim to belong to the generation; it made those who didn't qualify wish to belong as well. In its many variations, it sounded a note of individual rebellion, of a determination to work outside conventional securities: Hemingway's Nick Adams makes a "separate peace"; Dos Passos' John Andrews calmly accepts the penalties of desertion; Floyd Dell's heroes and heroines run the gamut, from Iowa to Chicago to Greenwich Village; and Lieutenant Henry speaks for them all:

That was what you did. You died. You did not know what it was about. You never had time to learn. They threw you in and told you the rules and the first time they caught you off base they killed you.

The range of experience varies, the definition achieves different shades and degrees of meaning. But the prevailing impression is that of the very young, frightened and puzzled and defeated at the start, but determined to formulate a code that both justifies and utilizes that defeat. This was part of the tone of the 1920s: a rhetorical quality quite different from the gestures made by Frank Norris's trapped superman or Theodore Dreiser's Hurstwood. It was a pathos realized too early, with neither the setting nor the incentive to give it the quality usually associated with "tragedy."

As for the attitude of the "unregenerate bohemian," it was even more roundly condemned by those who later criticized the decade, because it apparently ignored altogether what was usually recognized as "social experience." Far from being depressed by the period of his birth, the bohemian preferred to ignore it, except in satirical acknowledgment of its absurdity. The individual became an uncompromising anarchist, a radical of a kind that has almost vanished from the American scene since 1930. There were two variations of this attitude: one assumed that the aesthetic and the social conscience were the same; the other assumed there was no such thing as a social conscience, that there was no history but only persons. It was natural enough that this latter view should condemn the type of middle-class person Cummings had scornfully called the "official." Upton Sinclair proved to be the sole active survivor of progressive liberalism in the twenties, and Cummings was almost alone in his active sponsorship of aesthetic radicalism in the thirties. To affirm the value of the non-social personality was a difficult and unpopular task after 1929; even Maxwell Bodenheim marched in proletarian parades up Fifth Avenue in the thirties. But the basic point of view stated and dramatized in *The Enormous Room* was never altered thereafter by Cummings, except in details and kinds of reference.

Throughout the twenties writers shifted their ground uncomfortably with respect to the question of their debt to society. Of this maneuvering we have abundant evidence in Joseph Freeman's *An American Testament* and in the early history of the *New Masses*. But the position taken by Cummings is a partial sign of what in the decade was thought to be a most important privilege: that of aesthetic self-determination. From this point of view, most attacks were launched, trivial or profound or both, upon the restrictions and conventions of the world. The aesthetic radical retained a free and independent mind, refusing to permit any interference with his freedom. He was flattered to think that his views might be explained "scientifically," but he rejected without qualification the basic requirements of a scientific method. More often than not the "unregenerate bohemian" rejected philosophy as such altogether, thought himself possessed of finer instincts than the "prurient philosophers" of Cummings' poem.

The unregenerate bohemian was an extreme form of what has been an important contribution to modern culture: the emphasis, the *insistence*, upon the value of personal vision. The 1920s were one of a very few times when one could be respected for having a private view of public affairs. This private view applied not only to actual headline copy but to systems of philosophical thought, to scientific discoveries, to investigations of the nature of man and his world, and to theories of the writing and value of literature.

Much of the activity thus sponsored was of course reckless and irresponsible in its neglect of logic and in its sporadic enthusiasms. Nevertheless the literary activity of the decade stressed the very defensible assumption that the artist's sensibility is a legitimate means of gaining insight and knowledge that are indispensable to our total view of a culture. Since the artists of the decade realized the importance of their gift, they gave a special quality of insight into facts often unchallenged or misunderstood by others. For one thing, they pointed, not to the gifts of science, but to its dangers. They risked being called frivolous and ignorant, so that they might point out that science was not wholly good, that material progress may even be quite harmful, that an entirely satisfactory religious experience was all but impossible in a world that had "educated" itself beyond the need of it.

Perhaps their strongest (at any rate their loudest) activity consisted of their documentation of human absurdities. This criticism of the modern world, in spite of its frequent triviality, was both a profound and a necessary contribution to the knowledge we must have of our society. We realize now that for the most part it was correct and shrewd. Its value can be seen in several ways. One is its treatment of history, the act of taking the straight line of liberal prophecy and twisting it—rejecting the linear view of H. G. Wells for the cyclical view of Spengler. Another is the valuable distinction often drawn between scientific data and aesthetic—which suggested that mere science omitted much from what Ransom called "the world's body," and warned that a too narrow concern with abstract principle is almost as bad for life as it is for art. Again, this generation of critics described what they called a loss of taste in contemporary life. Vulgarity was clearly defined as a frantic and amoral desire to accumulate and to own goods; further, as the feeling that taste might be bought and did not need to be a responsible part of experience as a whole. The absurdities of the bourgeois mind and soul, the deformities of its architecture and its conscience, were never so fully documented. Perhaps the most valuable criticisms of the decade, and the most profound, were those which made it clear that defections of taste were not merely surface phenomena but betrayed an underlying inadequacy in our tradition and our culture.

These criticisms could not, after all, have remained effective had they pointed merely to superficial issues. The 1920s could make no more important contribution than is contained in their most jealously guarded thesis: that history and society are and remain abstractions until they are associated with personal experience. As Arthur Mizener has said (*Kenyon Review*, Winter 1950):

> . . . the situation, the moment in history, is not in itself tragic; it only provides the occasion on which the aware individual suffers the experience of unavoidable moral choices. No matter what the occasion, there is no tragedy where the forces of circumstance are not transmuted into personal experience.

If the twenties in America can be condemned seriously for a fault, it is not for their vulgarity (there is vulgarity of some sort in any time) or for their immorality (immorality in any period is ordinarily a characteristic of the move toward moral redefinition). The greatest fault was their naïveté. Men and women were often quite literally and self-avowedly ignorant of tradition. They had chosen to be; they had rejected both sound and unsound generalities and thought. As a result they were open to every new influence that came along; in most cases there was no intellectual experience to use as a measure of validity. That is undoubtedly the reason so much of the discussion of ideas in the decade seemed the talk of an undergraduate newly and overly impressed by his introductory course in philosophy. . . .

It is perhaps unfortunate that we know so much and are so helpless at the same time. In looking back upon the 1920s perhaps we ought not to be worried about the "party we cannot afford to throw again," but rather about our loss of confidence in free, if erratic, inquiry, which we seem to have abandoned along with our naïveté. Our knowledge seems to lack the strength of will that accompanied the ignorance and the errantry of the 1920s. We become more sophisticated and more inflexible with each passing year. We are competent scholars, writers, thinkers, voters; we are properly shocked when one of our fellows commits an especially noticeable error against good taste and good manners. Why, then, are we restless, uncertain, and unhappy? Why is our literature not first-rate? Why are the majority of our critical essays written about the literature of the 1920s and not about that of our own time? Something must be true of that decade that has nothing to do with the big party they were supposed to have had. Perhaps they were more sane, less frivolous, than we have been led to believe.

"THE USES OF INNOCENCE"

The positive values of the 1920s may perhaps best be suggested in the phrase "useful innocence." In the decade two generations collaborated in an exhaustive review of America's past greatness and present status. The one, the "old generation," contemporary with the Old Gang, surveyed the weaknesses of a tradition that had culminated in a war and an uneasy peace. The other generation, young in 1920 but old enough to have attended or participated in the ceremonies of 1914–1918, assumed the task of renewing that culture, of making it over according to new principles and what seemed newly acquired insights into human nature.

Of necessity, many of the writings of the decade were either important variants of old forms or new and original forms. No one can overemphasize the value of formal experiment in the 1920s. De Voto and Brooks have complained about "moral failure" and the "literary fallacy." The truth is that the writers of the 1920s, finding a world that seemed cut free of the past, had to invent new combinations of spirit and matter and new forms of expressing the human drama. They were not aided by any secure ordering of social or religious systems. They were novelists of manners in a society distrustful of past definitions, poets of formalized insight into moral chaos. Their restless desire for the new was always motivated by their distrust of the old. *Form*, then, was a major concern, a major necessity. The careers of all important writers who began publishing in the decade are marked by a restless concern with literary form. Since the forms of the past had been generally associated with a tradition now abhorred, the new forms had perforce to be different, newly inspired, and newly seen.

When Gertrude Stein lectured on method, when Ezra Pound fulminated against softness and weakness of speech, they were speaking for a formal revolution that was also a moral revolution. The concern with form was basically a concern over the need to provide an aesthetic order for moral revisions. It is true that the best of our writers were preoccupied with literature; they were "whole men" in the genuine sense of being profoundly concerned with the moral value of literary form. Essential to the enlightenment the decade gave us was that sense of the significance of the aesthetic, of its essential nature. Such a preoccupation appears on the surface to be morally irresponsible; actually it is truly moral in the sense of its earnest desire to communicate the variants of the modern condition.

The great strength of the decade lay in its useful and deliberate innocence. Ideas habitually lose their vitality as the employment of them alters or is too closely aligned with social expediency. Naïve, innocent demonstrations of wrath over smugness, indolence, or hypocrisy are outward expressions of moral revision. The language communicates these ideas; when they descend from the level of genuine moral judgment to that of comfortable journalism, the language and the forms must be changed. The writers of the 1920s, concentrating on literary form, went about the business of morally redefining the function of the language and its association with present realities. To begin with the "new"—which is to say, the raw, unformed, unsupported, and unexplained present literary condition—is to begin innocently afresh, to explore "the thing seen" in terms of the "way it is seen."

Having rejected all precedents, the writers of the 1920s themselves became precedents for the literature of future decades. But it was in their literary, their aesthetic, successes that future writers saw merit. The narrator of Budd Schulberg's *The Disenchanted* (1950) wishes that he could accept the brilliant literary successes of Halliday and ignore the *man* who had achieved them. This narrator is a *naïf* of another decade, unable to see the tragic artist whole or judge him from any point of view other than the documentary morality of the 1930s. It is almost beyond the capacity of those who look at the 1920s, however carefully, to understand the close rapport between literary concentration and moral insight. The writers of the 1920s—or many of them—had both to *see* a world as it frankly was and to *re-establish* that world in their literary formulations. The very matter of Fitzgerald's moral extravagances (which are the substance of Halliday's past) is incorporated into his art; however imperfectly, that art formalized what would otherwise have been merely a series of sensational and superficial dissipations. The writers of the 1920s believed in everything, those of the 1930s in only one thing, those of the 1940s in nothing. The second and third groups borrowed from the first the means of formulating their one thing and their nothing. This fact startlingly, enduringly remains: the 1920s were an opportunity and a challenge offered to a group of persons who were freshly and naïvely talented, anxious to learn *how* to restate and redramatize the human condition, morally preoccupied with the basic problem of communicating their insights into their present world.

But the weight of tradition is always heavy upon the individual talent. The important truth of the decade is not that its artists rejected the past but that they looked at the past from an orientation psychologically different from that of previous decades. They did not borrow from tradition so much as they forced tradition to give to them precisely what they needed from it. They refused to accept without question the formal systems of judging and dramatizing the moral values of the human race, preferred to select what they would, and on their own terms, from what the past had to offer. As a result the literary history of the decade, like its moral history, is a mélange of contrivance, experiment, and revolt.

Invariably didactic precedent interferes with a genuine moral appraisal of such a time and such a phenomenon. The literary heroes of the time assist in perpetuating the confusion: they recant, they are "converted," they rebel against their rebellion, they grow old and do not dare to face impeachment. They cannot see, or do not wish to see, that what they did and were at one time was of the utmost importance for the state of their own health and of that of society at large.

This fact, that they do not now wish

to see and that no one cares truly to see for them, remains of all the important positive legacies of the decade: the fact of useful innocence. They were truly, recklessly, innocently, rawly, tenaciously naïve. The emperor had worn no clothes after all. The world had not been saved. The health of society was not after all good. The Bridge did not lead us to Cathay. They therefore made—formally, aesthetically, and morally—what they could of the thing that they had seen. They often crossed the Atlantic in an attempt to see it from another perspective, to disengage themselves from its immediate nature only to see it more closely. They went to masters of French poetry, of seventeenth-century British drama, of nineteenth-century German philosophy and psychology, and took from them what "influences" they needed. But the best of them were from the beginning, and remained, endowed with talent, with reserves of irony, satire, and intelligent respect for the "right word." The best of them preserved in their work the exact *rapprochement* of experience with the act of experiencing, of action with the moral comedy of man acting.

When, as almost always, men complain of the 1920s that there was no steady adherence to the morally proper, they are narrowly right but fundamentally wrong. This was no time for Edith Wharton, as she admitted; in a genuine sense the opportunity for a formalized comedy of social manners had passed, and with it the opportunity to employ a fixed, traditional mode of moral examination. François Mauriac once said that if one were asked what is the most genuinely real human experience of personal agony, he would have to answer that it is the time immediately preceding his death, when the full weight of tradition and personal past bears upon an uncertain future, immediately foreseen. The moment of one's death is of such primary importance that the history of an entire culture can be relevant to it. This crisis in human experience requires all moral strength to meet it. But no one has sufficiently explored the role that form plays at such a time. The "comforts" that a culture offers then are either extremely reassuring or vaguely disturbing. When, as occurs so often in the literature of the 1920s, men say that "it does not mean anything to die," they would like to suggest that the agony of death is not attended by the solaces of a public moral security. It is indispensable to the health of any culture that this security be constantly examined, naïvely questioned, explosively rejected, and finally re-established and re-formed.

The "best of them" who did not die in 1914–1918, who came back to "frankness as never before," were possessed of a useful innocence in their approach to the world that was left them. They explored the corridors of history, inspected the meaning of a religion temporarily discredited; they formulated in several brilliant ways the most important of all symbolic figurations of our century—that of isolation, of the single, dispossessed soul whose life needs to be reestablished in terms specifically new and unencumbered. They did not always succeed in defining this symbol, for themselves or for others. Many of their works suffered from intellectual colloquialism—which, like all other forms of colloquialism, loses its value as it loses its fresh relevance. But the great contributions to our ways of speaking about our ways of feeling have—in a manner still and always valuable—preoccupied themselves with the proper answers to the question Eliot's Gerontion put to himself at the beginning of the decade: "After such knowledge, what forgiveness?" After such experiences, what forms remain of meeting, defining, and sensibly tolerating the human condition?

III. A FINAL EVALUATION OF THE DECADE'S INTELLECTUAL DISCONTENT

Henry Steele Commager (1902–)

THE LITERATURE OF REVOLT

As a social historian, Henry Steele Commager has shown a strong proclivity to investigate the nation's cultural past. He is sympathetic with the literary artists of the twenties and their protests against social injustices and the loss of individualism. He realizes that their artistic sensibilities would not allow them to accept the ugliness of the business world, but he does not believe that their alienation from society lead them to make false criticisms. However, Commager criticizes them for a failure to give their readers any positive guidelines or means for resolving the collective dilemma.

IN THE mid-twenties a distinguished historian described American civilization as "almost wholly a businessman's civilization." Perhaps the generalization had been valid since Appomattox, but its validity was more readily conceded in a decade when the president announced that the business of America was business and when a political campaign could substitute the promise of two cars in every garage for the more modest full dinner-pail of an earlier generation. The advertisers, the radio, the movies, popular journals and newspapers, even churchmen, hastened to welcome the "new era," and colleges and universities were zealous to confer their honorary degrees upon corporation lawyers and stockbrokers. A chorus of praise for what was now, in spite of Jefferson, called the American system ascended to the skies. No major novelist joined in the chorus: the novelists remained unreconciled and unregenerate.

Yet the direct assault of the Populist-Progressive era was abandoned. Muckraking had been played out, and there were no successors to *The Arena* or *McClure's* or *Hamptons,* or to Herrick and Churchill and Phillips and Whitlock. It was partly that, as William Allen White later recalled, "the whole liberal movement . . . which had risen so proudly under Bryan and Roosevelt and LaFollette, was tired. The spirits of the liberals . . . were bewildered." It was partly that the public, lulled into complacency by prosperity and disillusioned by the abortive crusade to make the world safe for democracy, was no longer interested in exposures. It was chiefly that the triumph of business was so spectacular and its battlements were so formidable, that it seemed invulnerable to direct assault. Protest perished, but the attack, in so far as that term may be used, was oblique and insidious. It took the form of satire and of repudiation, and satire and repudiation are confessions of defeat.

The confession is written large in the literature of the twenties. For as the novelists contemplated the business civilization which reached its apogee in that decade they were uncomfortable

From *The American Mind* by Henry Steele Commager, pp. 260–267, 273–276. Reprinted by permission of Yale University Press.

rather than indignant, derisive rather than rebellious; their protest was personal and their estrangement private. They looked with disapproval, even scorn, upon the contemporary scene, but they confessed no sense of shock, only a desire to shock. And what was perhaps most striking about the fiction which they wrote was not its overtones of satire and its undertones of antipathy and repudiation, but that the satire should be directed toward the middle classes rather than toward the rich, that the antipathy should be reserved for the social rather than the economic manifestations of the new era, and that the repudiation should be private rather than public. What these novelists lacked was what their predecessors so conspicuously had—sympathy, dignity, and purpose. They were not deeply moved by wrong because they had so little pity for the victims of wrong. They were not outraged by the violation of moral standards because they themselves were so unsure of their standards. They did not embark upon crusades because they had no program, only an attitude. They did not stand at Armageddon and battle for the Lord—how could they when they did not believe in the Lord?—but fled to Greenwich Village or to the Left Bank and thumbed their noses at the middle classes or at Puritanism or at the small town. Their greatest ambition was *épater la bourgeoisie,* their greatest triumph when the bourgeoisie acknowledged the shock.

Yet that triumph was brittle and evanescent. The economic hide was too thick for the barbs of the satirists, and the ultimate evidence of the futility of the attack was the enthusiasm with which it was welcomed by its victims. How completely mere satire failed of its purpose was made clear in the case of Sinclair Lewis, for when the public swarmed to buy his novels, when Main Street became a national shrine and Babbitt a folk hero, when the Pulitzer Committee found that *Arrowsmith* reflected the "wholesome atmosphere of American life," the joke was surely on Lewis himself rather than on Gopher Prairie or Zenith. Others who took refuge in satire or in malice suffered a comparable fate: the mordant Ring Lardner was regarded as a first-rate sports writer; the profoundly disillusioned Fitzgerald was acclaimed the spokesman for gilded youth; James Branch Cabell, whose repudiation of contemporary life was complete, achieved popularity because Jurgen contained passages esoterically erotic; Mencken, whose hatred of democracy was morbid, was embraced by all the young liberals; *The New Yorker* was welcomed as merely a humorous magazine, the fortunate successor to *Life* and *Judge*.

Of all the novelists of the twenties, it was Sinclair Lewis who gave the most elaborate report on his society and whose scenes and characters came most nearly to symbolize its meaning to the future. *Main Street* was published the year of Howells' death, and its author was, as much as any one could be, Howells' successor. Yet the contrasts between Howells and Lewis are more striking than the similarities. Both were observant and shrewd, both ranged widely over the national scene though rarely outside the middle classes they knew so well, both were realists and critics. Both were historians of the commonplace, but where Howells had rejoiced in the commonplace, Lewis found it intolerable. Both were interested primarily in character, but where Howells was concerned with its inner compulsions, Lewis was content with its outward manifestations. Both looked with skepticism upon the conventions of their day, but where Howells acquiesced in order to achieve intellectual freedom, Lewis battered so frantically against convention that he had no energy left to enjoy the freedom he won. Where Howells was urbane, Lewis was raucous; where he was judicious, Lewis was dogmatic; where he was affectionate—or at least compassionate—Lewis was scornful. Yet Howells' quarrel with his society was deeper than Lewis', his repudiation more fundamental.

For in this, too, Lewis mirrored his age, that he was content with surface effects, with photographs that were merely candid, with passion that was merely verbal. He belonged to that school of historians content with description and not curious to know the causes of things. Sooner or later he turned his searchlight on almost every aspect of American society and on almost every problem that engaged public attention, but a searchlight illumines only the surface of what it touches. He left few areas of American life unexplored but none surveyed, few issues unprobed but none explained: how futile, after all, were Babbitt's gestures toward emancipation, how irrelevant to the problem of religion the chronicle of Elmer Gantry's sleazy antics, how inconclusive the struggle of Arrowsmith for professional integrity. Like so much of the liberalism of the twenties, Lewis' protest was literally inconsequential.

Although it is clear that Lewis disapproved of the society and economy of his day, it is never quite clear what kind of society or economy would command his approval. He was in revolt, but his revolt was against bad manners rather than bad morals, and we feel that he found bigotry intolerable not so much because it maimed its victims as because it was an outward manifestation of smugness. His mimicry was devastating, his rage immense, but he never found an object wholly worthy of so much passion, and the rare victories his characters win over their mean environment—some brief emancipation, some glimpse of beauty, some lapse into decency—move us as little as the defeats and humiliations they suffer. He is for the most part the historian of defeat, yet if there are few happy endings in his books, there are few that are tragic, for he does not allow his characters the dignity of tragedy. Though he differed wholly from H. L. Mencken in philosophy, he was, like Mencken, engaged in guerrilla warfare against the *boobus Americanus,* and his novels were an extended gloss on those American Creeds that drag their dreary way through the pages of the old *American Mercury.*

It is in *Babbitt* that we find the most extensive report on society in the twenties, and the contrast between Howells and Lewis can best be appreciated when we compare Silas Lapham with George Babbitt. Silas Lapham, for all his vanity, his weakness, his vacillation, his confusion, is a hero. He has dignity, integrity, and character. The battles he fights are real, like the Civil War battles in which he was wounded—the battle for his farm, for his factory, for his family, for his own integrity; the victories he wins, the defeats he suffers, are meaningful. Nor is the society in which he moves negligible, or the delicate issues of class relationships, business honesty, friendship and love. But what shall be said of Babbitt—that "walking corpse" as Parrington calls him—content with his dull life, his dull family, his dull house, his dull business, his dull town, his dull ideas, his dull virtues and duller vices, mouthing the platitudes of the Rotary Club and the Republican platform as if they were gospel? What but that he is not only a success, but the very symbol of Success, the symbol of the New Era. Babbitt is a caricature who came to life; here, as so often, nature conformed to art.

With the passing of years Gopher Prairie and Zenith took on something of the charm of period pieces and—by comparison with the Grand Republic of *Cass Timberlaine* and *Kingsblood Royal*—a certain dignity. The society described in *Main Street* and *Babbitt* is shabby but rarely vicious, numbered a few honest men and women, and recognized some standards of morality. Not so that reconstructed by Ring Lardner. He, too, transcribed the American dream of success, but with him the dream was a nightmare. The dreadful specimens who haunt his pages are both shabby and vicious: the hopeless provincials who yearn for the Big Town, the moronic baseball players headed for the bush leagues, the sadistic prize fighters ready to sell out, the dopes and chumps, the crooks and chiselers and their gullible victims, the drummers with their appalling stories, the ham actors who dream of Broadway, the golfers who cheat and the caddies who lie, the illiterates who think they can earn a fortune writing poetry for the papers, the butter-

and-egg men whose love nests are charnel houses, the "Mr. and Mrs." always suspicious, always quarreling, always avaricious. Lardner sears them all with impartial hatred.

A universal avarice corrodes and consumes all his victims: it is their one positive trait. They know neither love nor passion nor tenderness; they have no interests, no ideas, no conversation, even. They are interested only in Success, and Success is money, not earned but chiseled. They know all the tricks for getting ahead: how to meet the right people, who are always the wrong people; how to make a good impression, which inevitably is a fatal one; how to get on the inside of a good thing, which invariably turns out to be a bad thing. They lie and cheat, gamble and swindle, bilk their associates and doublecross their wives and husbands. And always in vain.

For Lardner is above all the historian of frustration—of courtships that go on the rocks or, what is worse, end in marriage; of honeymoons that fizzle out, of marriages that turn sour; of plays that flop, prize fights that are fixed, games that blow up; of beauty that is skin deep, affection that is phony, talent that is meretricious. Thus his account of "How to Write Short Stories" closes with the recommendation that ambitious writers

> take up the life of a mule in the Grand Canyon. The mule watches the trains come in from the east, he watches the trains come in from the west, and keeps wondering who is going to ride him. But she never finds out.

The mule is a symbol for all Lardner's characters: they wait, and nothing happens, nor do they ever find out.

Nothing happens, nothing ever pans out; life is infinite boredom, futility, and frustration. It is the theme, too, of Scott Fitzgerald, the most gifted of all the novelists of the twenties, the incomparable historian of gilded youth, of the jazz age, of the rich and the near rich, of the great prosperity and the great disillusionment. His characters are, for the most part, extravagantly rich, but they differ from those of Lewis and Lardner chiefly in circumstances, not in aspirations: it is when we contrast Fitzgerald's playboys and demimondaines with their equivalents in Edith Wharton or Henry James that the comparison is qualitative. Nor do West Egg or the Riviera or Hollywood differ greatly from Gopher Prairie or Zenith or the Big Town, except that their inhabitants live what the hapless denizens of the sticks dream and thus reveal the tawdriness of the dream. Amory Blaine, penniless and jobless, his Rosaline deserting him for a richer man; Anthony Patch, heir to thirty millions, but broken by excesses and unbalanced by anxiety; the great Jay Gatsby bereft and murdered; the marionettes of *Tender Is the Night* indulging in aimless infidelities along the Riviera; Monroe Stahr smashed in an airplane before he could produce the kind of pictures he wanted—or call off the murder he had planned—how do they differ from George Babbitt or Jack Keefe except in the poignancy of their disillusionment?

First implicity in *This Side of Paradise,* then more explicitly in *The Beautiful and the Damned, The Great Gatsby,* and *Tender Is the Night,* and finally in the wonderful fragment of *The Last Tycoon,* Fitzgerald laid bare the pathology of that generation which Gertrude Stein had called "lost," and it is relevant to remember that pathology derives from pathos. His theme—as surely as that of Dos Passos—was the Big Money, and he showed, not with malice but with compassion, what money did to his generation, how its standards conditioned life, dictated habits, condemned to futility, and led, in the end, to that "crack-up" which he himself experienced. He is the chronicler of the Beautiful but especially of the Damned, of All the Sad Young Men, of the golden bowl of riches that was so fatally flawed.

Of all Fitzgerald's novels, *The Great Gatsby* best mirrors not so much the economy as the economic fantasies of the twenties. Here, in the curious blend of Jay Gatsby's fancies and attainments, was the dream life: education at Oxford (which college was it, now?); a tour of "all the capitals of Europe—Paris, Venice, Rome, collecting jewels, chiefly rubies, hunting big game, painting a little"; a majority in the Army; decorations from every Allied government, "even little Montenegro"; and then a business in New York (what matter if it was disorderly?) and an estate on Long Island. Here was the dream mansion at West Egg: its feudal silhouette, its marble steps, its "Marie Antoinette music rooms and Restoration salons, its period bedrooms swathed in rose and lavender silk and vivid with new flowers, dressing rooms and poolrooms, and bathrooms with sunken baths," its bars stocked with Scotch and Rye, its swimming pool and private beach and private plane. Here was the dream car: "rich cream color, bright with nickel, swollen here and there in its monstrous length with triumphant hat-boxes and supper-boxes and tool-boxes, and terraced with a labyrinth of windshields that mirrored a dozen suns . . . a sort of green leather conservatory." *The Great Gatsby* is one of the saddest novels in American literature. It is not that, in the end, Gatsby lies dead in the symbolic swimming pool and the rooms of the fabulous mansion are silent; it is rather that while he lived he realized all his ambitions.

There was, it must be admitted, something a little plaintive about all this, just as there was something plaintive about the whole self-conscious postwar generation. "Lost, and forever writing the history of their loss," as Alfred Kazin observes, "they became specialists in anguish. They had the charm of the specially damned." The satire in which Lewis and Lardner indulged, the bright depravity of Fitzgerald, the whimsy of Van Vechten, the flight from reality of Hergesheimer and Thornton Wilder and Elinor Wylie, were like one of the nervous breakdowns these novelists so often recorded—a luxury denied to farmers or washwomen and reserved for the sophisticated and the rich. There was, even at the time, something precious about their repudiation of a society whose dullness and meanness they exploited so successfully and which rewarded them so well: Fitzgerald himself admitted of his Jazz Age that he

> looked back to it with nostalgia. It bore him up, flattered him and gave him more money than he had dreamed of, simply for telling people that he felt as they did, that something had to be done with all the nervous energy stored up and unexpended in the war. . . . It all seems rosy and romantic to us who were young then. (*Echoes of the Jazz Age*) . . .

Surveying the literature of the twenties, one of the most astute critics, Bernard De Voto, charged that the major novelists were victims of a literary fallacy—the fallacy that what they saw was the whole of America and that their report on it was faithful:

> The repudiation of American life by American literature during the 1920's signified that writers were isolated or insulated from the common culture. There is something intrinsically absurd in the image of a literary man informing a hundred and twenty million people that their ideals are base, their beliefs unworthy, their ideas vulgar, their institutions corrupt, and, in sum, their civilization too trivial to engage that literary man's respect. That absurdity is arrogant but also it is naive and most of all it is ignorant. For the repudiation was the end-product of systems of thinking, and the systems arose in an ignorance that extended to practically everything but imaginative literature and critical comment on it. (*The Literary Fallacy*, p. 150)

Mr. De Voto, in short, was pained that the novelists did so badly by American civilization, that they emphasized its harrowing aspects and ignored its admirable. He wrote in 1944 when Americans, confronted with the greatest crisis of their history, had revealed qualities not wholly ignoble, and he asked how it happened that the walking shadows who strutted and fretted their hours through the pages of Lewis and Fitzgerald and Dos Passos were able to meet that crisis.

And it was, in fact, remarkable, a reflection on the accuracy of the literary interpretation. Yet Mr. De Voto's charge is a point of departure rather than a conclusion. No major critic denied that the novelists of the twenties and the thirties were alienated from their society: it is the theme of much of the writing of Edmund Wilson, of Lewis

Mumford, of Maxwell Geismar and Alfred Kazin. What is important is to ask how this situation came about. How did it happen that novelists from Lewis to Steinbeck were uniformly critical of America's business civilization? How did it happen that, after Silas Lapham, almost the only respectable businessmen in American fiction are Booth Tarkington's Plutocrat—the dubious Earl Tinker—and Sinclair Lewis' equally dubious Sam Dodsworth? Mr. De Voto is inclined to blame the novelists, and his resentment against what appears to be calculated misrepresentation is not hard to understand. Yet it is difficult to believe that all the novelists were blind except those who wrote for the popular magazines, that two generations of writers could have been led astray. It is, after all, a serious reflection on the business civilization that it was unable to commend itself to artists who were, on the whole, men of good will. . . .

Was American society, then, so much less admirable than the British in its economic manifestations? Was its cupidity more ostentatious, its irresponsibility more reckless, its cruelty more revolting? Was it afflicted with some singular depravity, ravished by some unique immorality? No one familiar with the economic history of the two countries would so argue. Indeed the most perspicacious British observers, from Bryce to Brogan, agreed that the American economy offered fairer rewards to the average man than any other in the world, and immigration statistics suggested that this opinion was widespread.

What then is the explanation of the minority report which imaginative writers filed on the American economy? It explains nothing to say that they were out of touch with reality: they had taken out a patent on realism. Perhaps it was that American economy had developed so rapidly and so spasmodically that it left little room for the amenities and the artist was more sensitive than others to ugliness. Perhaps it was that the transformation of a rural to an urban economy had been too abrupt and the artist, whose roots in the past were intellectual as well as personal, had failed to make the readjustment. Perhaps it was the novelists were, almost by nature, protestants: those who were content rarely bothered to write novels to advertise their felicity. Perhaps it was that the novelists, after all, were idealists, that they took seriously the promise of American life, expected to realize the American dream. They were not put off by the shibboleth of free enterprise, for they knew that the great tradition was the tradition of free men. "We must strike once more for freedom," wrote the youthful Dos Passos, "for the sake of the dignity of man." And that was what concerned most of those who addressed themselves to social and economic issues—not, perhaps, Faulkner or Caldwell or Lardner but the major figures from Howells to Steinbeck—freedom and the dignity of man. Thomas Wolfe spoke for them all in almost the last thing that he wrote:

> I believe that we are lost here in America, but I believe we shall be found. . . . I think the true discovery of America is before us. I think the true fulfillment of our spirit, of our people, of our mighty and immortal land, is yet to come. I think the true discovery of our own democracy is still before us. And I think that all these things are certain as the morning, as inevitable as noon. I think I speak for most men living when I say that our America is Here, is Now, and backons on before us, and that this glorious assurance is not only our living hope, but our dream to be accomplished. (*You Can't Go Home Again*)

Arthur M. Schlesinger, Jr. (1917–   )

THE REVOLT OF THE INTELLECTUALS

The son of a prominent historian, Professor Schlesinger has shown a particular interest on the history of reform movements from the Jacksonian era to the New Deal. His liberal views prompted President John F. Kennedy to seek him out as an adviser in 1961. Schlesinger's liberal democratic stance is evident in this account of the intellectual malaise of the twenties. He believes that the artists' alienation from a business society contributed to their sense of an indifferent universe and banished the expectations they had hoped to fulfill.

BUT the intellectual malaise went deeper than simply the exhaustion of liberalism. Only a minority of intellectuals, and those mostly the older, earnest men who remembered the New Nationalism and the New Freedom, retained much concern about America as a democratic society. The new generation had grown up, their spokesman said, "to find all Gods dead, all wars fought, all faiths in man shaken"; all they knew, wrote Scott Fitzgerald, was that "America was going on the greatest, gaudiest spree in history." It was an era of enchantment, where everything was rosy and romantic, where diamonds were as big as the Ritz, where for a brief decade, as Fitzgerald saw it, the wistful past and the fulfilled future seemed mingled in a single gorgeous moment.[1]

"It was characteristic of the Jazz Age," said Fitzgerald, "that it had no interest in politics at all." It was an age of art, of excess, of satire, of miracle; but who was to care about economics, when business policy seemed so infallible? Or about politics, when business power seemed so invincible? If pressed, the young writer might confess himself an anarchist, devoted to the freedom of the individual, hostile to censorship and prohibition and Babbittry; but politics—So what, Oh yeah, No, Nah. "I decline to pollute my mind with such obscenities," said George Jean Nathan. ". . . If all the Armenians were to be killed tomorrow and if half the Russians were to starve to death the day after, it would not matter to me in the least." "If I am convinced of anything," said H. L. Mencken, "it is that Doing Good is in bad taste." Sending money to starving children in Europe, suggested Joseph Hergesheimer, was "one of the least engaging ways in which money could be spent." "I burn with generous indignation over this world's pig-headedness and injustice," said James Branch Cabell, "at no time whatever."[2]

It was not that they had any use for the business civilization. They hated it; but, while hating it, they accepted it basically at the businessman's own evaluation—accepted it, that is, as a successful system, believed that it was working. Yet it remained for them stifling and repellent. The money madness, as a Chicago advertising man named Sherwood Anderson put it, was "beastly unclean." "America," wrote Kenneth Burke, a representative young intellectual of 1923, "is the purest concentration point for the vices and vulgarities of the

[1] Scott Fitzgerald, *This Side of Paradise* (New York, 1920), 304; "Early Success," *The Crack-Up*, Edmund Wilson, ed. (New York, 1945), 87–90.

[2] Scott Fitzgerald, "Echoes of the Jazz Age," *Scribner's*, Nov. 1931; G. J. Nathan, *The World of George Jean Nathan*, Charles Angoff, ed. (New York, 1952), 201; Malcolm Cowley, "Twenty Years of American Letters," *New Republic*, March 3, 1937; Louis Kronenberger, "H. L. Mencken," *New Republic*, Oct. 7, 1936.

From *The Crisis of the Old Order 1919–1933* by Arthur M. Schlesinger, Jr., pp. 145–152, 504–505. Reprinted by permission of Houghton Mifflin Company, and William Heinemann, Ltd.

world."[3] Such a culture demanded defiance; but defiance took the form not of a challenge to its politics or economies, but of an explosion of creative energy.

There were various styles of accommodation. Some chose physical flight —to Greenwich Village, or to the primitivism of Mexico, or to the sophistication of Paris. And those who stayed in the United States had their own forms of flight. On a common level there was the pose of ineffectuality, the average man's defense against an aggressive social order, expressed in the popular images on which the people unloaded their humors and their doubts: Krazy Kat, happy and hopeful, but everlastingly hit by the inevitable brick; Harold Lloyd, ever beset; Keaton, ever baffled; above all, Chaplin as lonesome humanity defying a world which must eventually all but overwhelm him.

On a more literary level, the technique of accommodation through comedy produced satire and fantasy—Lardner, Kaufman, and Hart, or, in a different vein, Cabell, Hergesheimer. The greatest satirical *fantaisiste* of them all, Sinclair Lewis, created a Middle West, stocked it with unforgettable symbols of business domination, and fixed the image of America, not just for the intellectuals of his own generation, but for the world in the next half-century. Or accommodation through escape found Hemingway and Fitzgerald seeking images of grace, courage, and love in the money-ridden world. Or accommodation through revolt—Dreiser, filled with clumsy pity, or Dos Passos, laying bare American life with shallow strokes of a shining surgical knife.

II

The novel was the most available means of resolving sensitive man's relationship to insensitive society; and, in the nonpolitical atmosphere of the twenties, it had a special attraction. Even men whose happier medium was politics now turned to literature. Donald Richberg, it is true, had published novels before. "Writing down an incoherent revolt tends to strengthen it and to make it real," he once said; thus his book of 1911, *The Shadow Men,* a melodramatic indictment of speculation, helped start him on his reform career. But his book of 1922, *A Man of Purpose,* was far more troubled and unhappy, with its bitter attack on business and its pathetic hope for some spiritual infusion, some nobility of purpose, in American life.[4]

William C. Bullitt was another fugitive from politics in fiction. Too restless to lie long on the Riviera, Bullitt had married the widow of John Reed, the Harvard Communist, and plunged into the excitement of the twenties. Between consulting with Freud in Vienna, living magnificently by the Bosporus, and returning occasionally to see the New Era at first hand, he settled old scores in Philadelphia by publishing *It's Not Done* in 1926. It was an agreeable exercise in the comedy of manners, filled with aristocratic contempt for postwar life, where success was defined as futility on the upgrade. "I seem to see," observes one character, "a capering virgin heifer with a blue face, a yellow back, and a buttoned-down tail who nevertheless exudes perpetually a stream of immaculately conceived milk and answers to the name: America." In the end, one character observes, "All we have to look forward to is Raoul's world, I suppose, Communism." The next year Bullitt's fellow townsman Francis Biddle in his graceful novel *The Llanfear Pattern* drew a scathing picture of life "without gaiety and without earnestness, mechanical, content, indifferent."[5] And Biddle could not even console himself with Bullitt's expectations of the future.

[3] Anderson to Waldo Frank, Oct. 29, 1917, in Sherwood Anderson, *Letters*, H. M. Jones and W. B. Rideout, eds. (Boston, 1953), 18; in *Vanity Fair,* 1923, quoted by Malcolm Cowley in *Exile's Return* (New York, 1934), 118.

[4] Donald Richberg, *Tents of the Mighty* (Chicago, 1930), 25; Donald Richberg, *The Shadow Men* (Chicago, 1911); Donald Richberg, *A Man of Purpose* (New York, 1922), 301, 313, vi.

[5] W. C. Bullitt, *It's Not Done* (New York, 1926), 340, 371; Francis Biddle, *The Llanfear Pattern* (New York, 1927), 252.

III

But this mood of gentlemanly resignation was not enough for the younger generation. They found the stimulus they sought much more in Henry L. Mencken and his comedy of revolt. With his magnificent nonchalance, his superb polemical style, and his uproarious contempt for the business culture, Mencken expressed what they wished they could have thought up about the impossibility of American life. There emerged the portrait of a nation in which the businessman and the farmer—in Menckenese, the booboisie and the Bible—had enthroned puritanism and hypocrisy; where the man who liked *potage créole,* Pilsener beer, Rühlander 1903, Brahms, pretty girls, and serious fiction was being suffocated between the Rotarian and the peasant.

It was all very splendid and liberating. But there was in it, not fully perceived, a deeper implication. The cultural pressures against which Mencken inveighed in the name of individual liberty appeared to him on closer examination inseparable from democracy itself. His essays turned into sustained ridicule of the very idea of self-government. Prohibition, censorship, the Klan, whether backed by the swinish rich or by the anthropoid rabble, were the inevitable consequence of the democratic theory.

Democracy, after all, in the end came to nothing but the mob, which was sodden, brutal, and ignorant. "Politics under democracy," said Mencken, "consists almost wholly of the discovery, chase and scotching of bugaboos. The statesman becomes, in the last analysis, a mere witch-hunter, a glorified smeller and snooper, eternally chanting 'Fe, Fi, Fo, Fum.'" Democracy's dominating motive was envy, given the force and dignity of law; the technique was government by orgy, almost by orgasm; in essence, democracy was a combat between jackals and jackasses. "It has become a psychic impossibility for a gentleman to hold office under the Federal Union, save by a combination of miracles that must tax the resourcefulness even of God." Urging more gentlemen to enter politics made no more sense, said Mencken, than to argue that the remedy for prostitution was to fill the bawdyhouses with virgins.

Mencken's typical congressman? "A knavish and preposterous nonentity, half way between a kleagle of the Ku Klux Klan and a grand worthy of the Knights of Zoroaster. It is such vermin who make the laws of the United States." The civil service? "A mere refuge for prehensile morons." Public opinion? The immemorial fears of the mob, "piped to central factories . . . flavoured and coloured, and put into cans." Democratic morality? "When one has written off cruelty, envy and cowardice, one has accounted for nine-tenths of it." The great democratic leaders? These were the most intolerable of all: Bryan, the "Fundamentalist Pope"; T.R., the "national Barbarossa"; Wilson, "the self-bamboozled Presbyterian, the right-thinker, the great moral statesman, the perfect model of the Christian cad." Democracy as a theory? "All the known facts lie flatly against it."[6]

The example of Mencken was devastating. He made interest in social questions ludicrous and unfashionable, democracy itself defensible only as farce. And, while Mencken provoked violent opposition, very little of it concerned itself with his assault on democracy. Indeed, his most formidable critics were, if anything, more vehement than he in their repudiation of democracy. These were the New Humanists, who, rejecting equally the anarchic naturalism of Mencken, the sentimentality of the liberals, and the philistinism of the business community, sought to evoke for the Coolidge era an aristocratic philosophy of self-discipline, standards, *appamada,* the "inner check."

Irving Babbitt, the most influential of the New Humanists, objected to the whole modern movement of democracy. He doubted whether universal sufferage was compatible with the degree of safety for property which civilization

[6] H. L. Mencken, *Notes on Democracy* (New York, 1926), 9, 22, 106–7, 126, 137, 176, 192; H. L. Mencken, *Prejudices: Second Series* (New York, 1920), 102, 117; H. L. Mencken, *Prejudices: Fifth Series* (New York, 1926), 70.

required; and he had no use for the "sickly sentimentalizing over the lot of the underdog." A real statesman, said Babbitt, would have "died in his tracks" rather than sign, as had Wilson, the Adamson Act establishing an eight-hour day for railroad labor. Laissez faire was little better, making mill operatives mere cannon fodder in the industrial warfare. "The remedy for the evils of competition," said Babbitt, "is found in the moderation and magnanimity of the strong and the successful." And, while he did not pretend to be happy about the choice, circumstances might well arise, he said, "when we may esteem ourselves fortunate if we get the American equivalent of a Mussolini; he may be needed to save us from the equivalent of a Lenin."[7]

IV

What began as an alienation from business culture was ending in some cases as an alienation from democracy itself. And it was an alienation that provoked no exploration of social alternatives; for there seemed little point in seeking alternatives when the existing order seemed so permanent. Never before in American history had artists and writers felt so impotent in their relation to American society. The business culture wanted nothing from the intellectual, had no use for him, gave him no sustenance. And, once the first gust of creative revolt had blown out, writers themselves began to feel that their sources of vitality were drying up. By 1927, reported Fitzgerald, a widespread neurosis began to be evident; by 1928 even Paris seemed stifling, and the lost generation began to look homeward.

T. S. Eliot, the American poet who had moved to England, a Harvard classmate of Walter Lippmann and John Reed, of Heywood Broun and Hamilton Fish and Bronson Cutting, had perceived the tendency earlier in the decade.

What are the roots that clutch, what
  branches grow
Out of this stony rubbish? Son of man,
You cannot say, or guess, for you know only
A heap of broken images, where the sun
  beats,
And the dead tree gives no shelter, the
  cricket no relief,
And the dry stone no sound of water. . . .
I will show you fear in a handful of dust.[8]

Was this modern man's destiny—life in the valley of dying stars? shape without form, shade without color, gesture without motion? Two books of 1929 said that it was, and that modern man must come to terms with it.

Walter Lippmann had in his own life described the arc of American liberalism, from Socialism to the New Nationalism to the New Freedom to urbane analyses of public opinion and political psychology. It was a journey away from conviction; and the first chapter of *A Preface to Morals* was appropriately entitled "The Problem of Unbelief." The acids of modernity, Lippmann said, had destroyed the faith that human destiny was in the charge of an omnipotent deity. The test of maturity, he suggested, was when man understood this "vast indifference of the universe to his own fate"; and the problem was how mankind, now deprived of the great fictions, could meet the deep human needs which had made those fictions necessary.

His answer was a personal one—the recovery of moral insight, to be achieved first by disentangling virtue from the traditional religious and metaphysical sanctions, then by encouraging that growth into maturity which would render an authoritarian morality unnecessary. The mature man must take the world as it comes. He "would be strong, not with the strength of hard resolves, but because he was free of that tension which vain expectations beget." Defeat and disappointment

[7] Irving Babbitt, *Democracy and Leadership* (Boston, 1924), 205, 214, 288, 312. One of Babbitt's darker warnings perhaps deserves repetition: if man "succeeds in releasing the stores of energy that are locked up in the atom—and this seems to be the most recent ambition of our physicists—his final exploit may be to blow himself off the planet." (*Democracy and Leadership*, 143).

[8] T. S. Eliot, "The Waste Land," *Collected Poems, 1909–1935* (London, 1936), 61–77.

would not touch him, for he would be "without compulsion to seize anything and without anxiety as to its fate." Renouncing desire, he would renounce disillusion; renouncing hope, he would renounce despair. In the last sentences of the book, Lippmann summarized his ideal of modern man. "Since nothing gnawed at his vitals, neither doubt nor ambition, nor frustration, nor fear, he would move easily through life. And so whether he saw the thing as comedy, or high tragedy, or plain farce, he would affirm that it is what it is, and that the wise man can enjoy it."[9]

With less eloquence but with even more implacable logic, Joseph Wood Krutch reached similar conclusions. What preoccupied him in *The Modern Temper* was the evident disappearance of animal vitality in modern civilization. Somehow mind itself had reasoned away, one by one, all those fixed points with reference to which life could be organized; science had destroyed faith in moral standards, in human dignity, in life itself. In the view of modern man, wrote Krutch, "there is no reason to suppose that his own life has any more meaning than the life of the humblest insect that crawls from one annihilation to another." For races have been enfeebled by civilization as though by a disease; human virtues could be biologic vices. "Civilizations," said Krutch, "die from philosophical calm, irony and the sense of fair play quite as surely as they die of debauchery."

Krutch was more pessimistic than Lippmann. When civilization became decadent, its hope of rejuvenation lay with the barbarians, who might restore a primitive instinct for survival; possibly the Communists might be the modern equivalent of the Goths and Vandals and, in destroying civilization, would give it the vital energy to rise again. But such hopes would mean little to modern men. "The world may be rejuvenated in one way or another, but we will not. Skepticism has entered too deeply into our souls ever to be replaced by faith."[10]

[9] Walter Lippmann, *A Preface to Morals* (New York, 1929), 187, 229, 209, 329–30.

[10] J. W. Krutch, *The Modern Temper* (New York, 1929), 9, 45, 183, 247, 249.

Granville Hicks (1901–)

TRUMPET CALL

A one-time member of the Communist party, Granville Hicks has been an editor and critic. He criticizes many of the writers of the twenties because of what he views as their evasion of responsibilities. He considers John Dos Passos to be one of the only writers who attempted to come to terms with the problems of his society and change it. Hicks never accepted the view that the literary artist must slavishly serve the interests of ideology.

ERNEST Hemingway presents himself frankly as a representative of the lost generation. From his two novels and his short stories there emerges a sort of composite character, the Hemingway hero, whose story is, in its broad outlines, the story not merely of Hemingway's life but of the lives of a not inconsiderable group of his contemporaries. This Hemingway hero, though born in America, was from the first a passive rebel, avoiding the familiar forms of American upbringing and associating with individuals outside the ranks of middle-class respectability. Never sure of any code of values, he let himself drift, and in time he drifted into the war. As a soldier he did his work competently, not through any sense of duty and certainly not because of patriotism, but because it was simpler to go straight ahead than to try to dodge. The war intensified his distrust of conventional values and impressed him afresh with the difficulty of preserving individuality. He came out of the war anxious to simplify life and willing, for the sake of simplification, to sacrifice much that other persons valued. He could not keep himself from feeling, but he could minimize the outward evidences of emotion; he could not keep himself from thinking, but he could refuse to attach much importance to the results of thought. As skeptical of esthetic standards as of moral, quite indifferent to philosophy, he sought no elaborate rationalization of his attitude, but he had his own conception of the good life. He found his chief satisfactions in bodily activity. To fish, to ski, to watch a boxing match or a bull fight not only made it possible to stop thinking but also gave life that momentary intensification that seemed the only reward for living.

Hemingway has, as a matter of fact, two heroes: the autobiographical hero, whose spiritual history we have traced, and the hero that Hemingway is not but thinks he would like to be. He has written often of simple, uncritical barbarians—the tramps in "The Battler," the gunmen in "The Killers," and the peasant in "An Alpine Idyll"—whose lives he finds free from hypocrisy and from the muddy swirl of thoughts and emotions that accompanies the acts of so-called civilized men. But recognizing the dulness of such existences, he prefers men who combine direct and unrationalized action with a capacity for intense response to the events of life. He admires, therefore, men of the sporting world and bull-fighters in particular. "Nobody," says one of his characters, "ever lives their life all the way up except bull-fighters." Thus Hemingway proposes a kind of remedy for the disease of his generation: if all else fails, if social obligations lose their force, if the desire for success is dead, if all philosophies seem equally meaningless and all philosophers equally futile, action remains, not action for a cause but action for its own sake, the unthinking, unhesitating, and if possible hazardous exercise of the body.

But no one with any awareness of the problems facing Hemingway's generation can doubt that this concern with physical activity is an evasion of responsibility. Moreover, it is not, even for Hemingway, an entirely satisfactory evasion. The whole problem of values, which he is trying to escape, rises up to haunt him. What gives significance to *The Sun Also Rises* is the character of Jake, who exercises self-control when it is most important and most difficult, and who fights against self-pity and the consolation of lying dreams. If he were merely a drifter, whining over his misfortune, one would have no sense of the tragedy of his life. Nor is Frederic in *A Farewell to Arms* merely a drifter; he has been drifting, it is true, but the book describes the establishment of a relationship, presumably the first in his life, that has value for him and that he wants to endure, and it is the interruption of that relationship that makes the story tragic. Even the short stories about the arena, the prize-ring, and the race track are less concerned with instinctive actions than with displays of courage and fortitude.

When it serves his purposes, Hemingway reveals the values he accepts, but he refuses to consider their implications. It is significant that he never attempts to defend his Catholicism, as Eliot and the others do; he gives no reasons for his conversion to the Church, and what lies behind his conversion is only hinted at in his books. The truth is that, if he once tried to state and justify his position, he would have to repudiate his novels and stories, for he would be forced to see, and so would his readers, that in his fiction he has created an artificial environment for his characters. In order to avoid problems that he is unwilling to face, he isolates his people from the forces that have made them what they are. The sense of futility he describes is not an accident; the values he accepts have a wider significance than he attributes to them or they have no significance at all. The effectiveness of Hemingway's work depends not so much on his accurate account of the actions and words of such people as Jake, Lady Brett, and Frederic as on his suggestion of the implications of what they say and do. But his refusal to examine those implications and to try to understand them limits the value and importance of his fiction.

It seems unlikely that he will ever transcend his limitations. "The great thing," he says at the end of *Death in the Afternoon*, "is to last and get your work done and see and hear and learn and understand; and write when there is something that you know; and not before; and not too damned much after. Let those who want to save the world [save it,] if you can get to see it clear and as a whole. Then any part you make will present the whole if it's made truly. The thing to do is work and learn to make it." This statement might be interpreted so that any author, whatever his convictions, could accept it; but saving the world and seeing it clear and as a whole are not so unrelated as Hemingway supposes. In fact the connection is so close that his contempt for those who would save the world betrays his unwillingness to see it for what it is. The artist makes his contribution to the salvation of the world by seeing it clearly himself and helping others to do the same. But certainly he does not see it clearly if he is constantly running away from whatever frightens or worries or bores him. Hemingway says, "After one comes, through contact with its administrators, no longer to cherish greatly the law as a remedy in abuses, then the bottle becomes a sovereign means of direct action. If you cannot throw it, at least you can always drink from it." If, in other words, you are troubled by the world, resort to personal violence, and if personal violence proves, as it usually does, to be ineffective, undignified, and even dangerous, console yourself with drink—or skiing, or sexual intercourse, or watching bull-fights. There is a point at which retreat becomes surrender and evasion becomes impotence. *Death in the Afternoon* suggests that Ernest Hemingway may not be far from that point. . . .

As we have noticed, the young esthetes came in time to feel that it was sufficient "to write a poem, an essay, a story worth the trouble of reading to one's friends." Certainly much of the literature of the twenties is curiously esoteric. It is difficult, for example, to understand a poem of T. S. Eliot's unless one has read the books that Eliot has read; and not many people have. Much of the poetry of Eliot's followers is almost completely unintelligible if one has not lived a certain kind of life. And the criticism of such men as Yvor Winters, Dudley Fitts, and R. P. Blackmur resembles the impassioned quibbling of devotees of some game. Little groups of writers sprang up in Paris, New York, and Cambridge, each with its own symbols and allusions. On the basis of assumptions shared by a few friends the poet or critic could and did elaborate vastly ingenious structures.

Such a development was the not unpredictable result of the isolation of these writers from the activities and interests of the masses of the American people. They had, as we have seen, no functional relationship to any class in American society, and they quickly discovered that they could not impress their standards on others. So each went his private way, finding what consolation he could in the understanding and appreciation of his friends. Some of them, indeed, denied that even the understanding of friends was necessary. The little group of Americans associated with *transition* frankly proclaimed that the world of private meanings is the author's only true province. The revolution of the word accomplished the ultimate statement of individualism. Its adherents, accepting the logical consequences of the theory of self-expression, completely repudiated any idea of the author's responsibility to the reader and simply denied the existence of the problems that had been troubling American authors for generation after generation.

But there was another possibility. If the author found it rather tiresome to write only for the few friends who understood him, he might contemplate the creation of a whole class of responsive persons. It is easy enough to see what the existence of a true leisure class and a genuine leisure-class culture might mean to the young writers of the twenties and thirties. Since the World War there has been, within the framework of bourgeois society, no group that can command the loyalties of the writer. He seldom has much respect for the leaders of finance and industry, and he usually has only contempt for the complacent, standardized Babbitts. As for the insurgents, the reformers and liberals, the writer is quite likely to be out of sympathy with their aims and certainly he can have little confidence in their methods. But if there were a group of persons with "the ease and maturity of plants in a well-kept garden," how pleasant it would be to associate with them, how comforting to write about them, how stimulating to write for them!

Before the depression of 1929 the creation of a leisure class seemed altogether possible. For years, of course, there had been many wealthy people, and a certain number of people who lived in leisure. But during the period of rapid capitalist expansion fortunes were made and lost so rapidly that stratification could not take place. In time, however, the risks and opportunities diminished, and great fortunes could be more safely handed from generation to generation. As this happened, the number of persons who had no functional connection with the productive system inevitably grew. Even in the twenties, however, these leisured persons had not grown into a compact and orderly group, with a common body of ideals, ideas, and interests. But so great was the need of many of the younger writers that they could not wait; they had to force the growth of a leisure-class culture.

There were many signs of such an effort in the twenties. T. S. Eliot's acceptance of the British Church and State is the most obvious indication that certain sorts of writers were feeling the need of the support that a leisure class could give. But one can point also to the interest of other writers in ecclesiastical tradition and to the humanists' treatment of economic problems. Wilder, as has been noted, deals almost entirely with aristocrats. Wescott, describing the subject he would like to write on, gives an idealized picture of a leisure class. Tate and his young Confederates dream of the revival of the plantation aristocracy. Most of the members of Hemingway's lost generation find time to devote to sports and drinking because they live on unearned incomes. In the work of the novelists and poets we can see the growth of the ideal of the leisure class and in the work of the critics we can see the attempt to forge the requisite intellectual bonds.

The depression demonstrated the prematureness of these efforts. At first it was regarded merely as an irritating interruption, but in time its implications became obvious even to the blindest and most isolated of the younger writers. Many of them have tried to adapt themselves to the new situation. Wescott, as we have seen, has become alarmed at the apparent disintegration of his world and the consequent shattering of his hopes. In the *Hound & Horn,* once so esoteric in its interests, articles appear on capitalism, Jeffersonianism, and Russia. There is the case of Archibald MacLeish, whose earlier poetry rivaled Eliot's in the communication of the hopelessness and self-distrust of a generation. But MacLeish, like Eliot, wanted to escape from the limbo of futility. Essentially a romantic, he desired values to affirm and heroes to admire. After expressing for years his disillusionment, he tried to create heroes in *Conquistador*, an elegiac account of Cortes and his little army of veterans in Mexico. MacLeish turned to the past for the heroes of his poem. But now he is looking for heroes in the present, and looking for them in Wall Street. America, he says in an article in the *Saturday Review of Literature*, "requires of its governors a conception of capitalism in which a man can believe—which a man can oppose in his mind to other and no longer visionary conceptions." Thus he appeals to big business men to be his heroes and to provide him with values.

There are many other signs that in the coming years the effort of a certain number of writers will be devoted, not to the creation of a leisure-class culture, but to the development of a body of capitalist apologetics. After all, the writers of whom we have been speaking do depend on the capitalist system. A while ago, when all was going well, they could ignore that fact, but now most of them realize it very keenly. At present they content themselves with attacking the enemies of capitalism, the while they discuss plans for its modification and preservation. But if the situation grows worse and capitalism is still further imperiled, it is reasonable to suppose that a certain number of writers will take a more definite stand in its defense. Most of them will not, presumably, defend capitalism as such, but they will defend a set of doctrines that involve not merely the preservation but the consolidation and extension of capitalist power. They will, in short, become fascists.

There is an alternative. John Dos Passos was one of the Harvard poets, but he seems to have been less completely drugged than his companions by Baudelaire, Petronius, and the Old Howard. He could write typical undergraduate poems and stories; he could make the usual Harvard jibes at "long-haired ultra-socialism"; but he could not blind himself to the fact that "millions of men perform labor narrowing and stultifying even under the best conditions." As was natural he blamed industrialism. "Are we not like men crouching on a runaway engine?" he asked in 1916. "And at the same time we insensately shovel in the fuel with no thought as to where we are being taken."

His experiences in the war intensified his distrust of an industrial civilization, and increased his longing for some sort of sanctuary. "God!" cries the autobiographical hero of *One Man's Initiation*, "if there were somewhere nowadays where you could flee from all this stupidity, from all this cant of governments, and this hideous reiteration of hatred, this strangling hatred." But the war also fostered a conflicting desire, the desire to understand and change the system that made such horror possible. The two desires lived, side by side, during his travels in Spain, as recorded in *Rosinante to the Road Again*, and in the East, as recorded in *Orient Express*. We shall have to know much more than we do now to be able to explain why the desire to flee was weaker in Dos Passos than in most of his contemporaries. But it was, and eventually the desire to understand and to affect the world in which he lived triumphed.

It was not, however, until 1925, when he wrote *Manhattan Transfer*, that Dos Passos was quite willing to take a long look at the world he had hated and sometimes fled from. Since there was so much in American life that baffled and irritated and alarmed and interested him, he could not write a conventional novel, but built his book out of some two hundred episodes, dealing with fifty or sixty persons, recurring again and again to some and carrying them through several years, giving only the briefest glimpses of others. Uniting these many episodes, which tell of reporters, actresses, waiters, politicians, milkmen, lawyers, bootleggers, sailors, and housewives, there is a basic rhythm, an underlying movement—beginning, struggle, bewilderment, defeat. Dos Passos summoned all his powers of description, all his knowledge of character, and packed into one book a richness of life that pounds upon the reader's sense with all the irresistibility of the composite din that daily strikes the metropolitan ear. Yet, though he had achieved much, he had not achieved enough: the book suggests the complexity of city life, but it gives us few memorable characters; it leaves us with a sense of the drift of men and events, but it does not indicate the direction of the drift. What keeps the novel this side of greatness is the author's bewilderment, which is not unlike the bewilderment of Jimmy Herf, the character who comes closest to being Dos Passos' counterpart and spokesman. When Jimmy leaves New York, we feel with him a temporary sense of relief; but we know well enough that his departure is no real solution of his own problems and can have no bearing upon the problems of the other characters still struggling in the metropolitan wilderness. Based on a bitterness that finds no adequate expression, culminating in a retreat that is a confession of futility, *Manhattan Transfer* leaves us with only a recollection of isolated scenes and an impression that the author has seen but has not understood.

In the difference between Dos Passos' two plays, *The Garbage Man* and *Airways, Inc.*, we trace the change that makes *The 42nd Parallel* his next novel, so superior to *Manhattan Transfer*. *The Garbage Man*, in its attempt to reproduce the chaos of modern life and to catch the glamorous spectacle that it makes, is close to the former novel and ends quite as unsatisfactorily. *Airways, Inc.*, bad as its overambitiousness makes it, is a fighting play, free from romanticism and doubt. At last Dos Passos is willing to face America because he has faith that out of the squalid chaos a decent civilization may come. When one believes that the horrible can be defeated, when one has good reasons for that belief, feels it deeply as a challenge, acts upon it as a philosophy of life, then one need no longer think of flight.

It is in the spirit of *Airways, Inc.*, that Dos Passos has written *The 42nd Parallel* and *1919*. In these novels he tells the stories of a number of representative Americans in the years before, during, and immediately after the World War: an I.W.W., a stenographer, a publicity agent, an interior decorator, and a garage hand; a sailor, a minister's daughter, a Harvard liberal, an impulsive Texan, and a Jewish radical. Some of these characters are involved with others; some, at the end of *1919*, still pursue their solitary courses. What holds these narratives together is not any web of intrigue or chain of circumstance. These persons belong together because they are being swept along by the same forces, a fact that Dos Passos indicates by interrupting the story of one to tell the story of another, and emphasizes by making his reader aware of broad social movements in the background. To portray this background, to give us the fullest possible sense of the mass emotions and actions that lie behind the comparatively few lives he has singled out to describe, he employs three devices: in the "Newsreels" we find the raw material of history, the actual and undigested stuff of experience, out of which the narrative sections have been fashioned; "The Camera's Eye," with its impressionistic bits of autobiography, strengthens the effect of reality by suggesting that the author, too, has been part of what he describes; the portraits, records of human heroism, meanness, bewilderment, victory, defeat, set before us the gods, demigods, and devils of our time, and give the novels an epic scope.

But the particular devices Dos Passos uses are relatively unimportant. It is what the devices express that matters. The ten narratives, the innumerable newspaper extracts, the autobiographical passages, and the tabloid biographies are held together by the author's realization that all of us, sailors and stenographers, interior decorators and publicity agents, J. P. Morgan and Wesley Everest, Charles Proteus Steinmetz and Woodrow Wilson, have been moving steadily towards a great crisis. That is why he can treat his characters both as individual entities and as parts of a larger whole, why he can let us see and sympathize with their hopes and sufferings at the same time that we are conscious of the larger drama in which they are merely supers. All his powers of observation and understanding have been intensified. As the scientist's hypothesis sharpens his perceptions by giving him a principle of selection, so the concept of the class struggle and the trend towards revolution, deeply realized in the emotions and translated into action, has given Dos Passos a greater sensitiveness to the world about him. But it has done something more important than that: it has shown him the relations between apparently isolated events and enabled him to see the fundamental unity beneath the seemingly chaotic complexity of American life. And it has banished, at last, all the dismay and doubt that, subtly insinuating themselves despite his efforts to dispel them, at one time sapped the vitality of his imagination.

Dos Passos has grown steadily during the last decade, and there is no apparent obstacle to his continued growth. For whom of his contemporaries can the same claim be made? Not for Elizabeth Madox Roberts with her pretty little elegies; not for Glenway Wescott, looking the world over for his ideal people; not for Thornton Wilder, playing with his dolls; not for William Faulkner, spinning complex melodramas out of his neuroses; not for Ernest Hemingway, with his twin opiates, drink and bull-fighting. There is the tragedy of Hart Crane, who longed, perhaps more deeply than anyone else in his generation, to reveal in enduring lines the innermost significance of all that America is and has been. Sharing the despair and bewilderment of his generation, he resolutely strove to put all that behind him, and in *The Bridge* wrote a powerful affirmation of the intrinsic worth and the majestic destiny of his country. The stark determination of the man speaks in the sonorous lines, the subtle rhythms, the bold metaphors. But what, fundamentally, was Crane seeking to affirm? He perceived the beauty of such structures as Brooklyn Bridge; he was aware of the poetic treasure concealed in our history and legends; he recognized in the courageous comprehensiveness and simple idealism of Walt Whitman a worthy inspiration. Intuitively he knew that there existed forces that could bring about the triumph of all that he cherished in American life; but what those forces were he could not tell, and in the end his affirmations rested only on a vague mysticism. Continued creation on such a foundation was for him, clear-sighted as he was, impossible. Worn out by his struggles, broken by his defeat, the prey of neuroses such as are often the product of extreme individualism, he refused to strive any longer in a world that for him held no possibility of success.

The tragedy of Hart Crane is more apparent than the tragedies of some of his contemporaries, but scarcely different in kind. If there are harsh words to be said about such men as Eliot, Hemingway, and Faulkner, it is not because one cannot understand the reasons for their failures, nor because one is loath to pay tribute to their virtues, but because the futility of the ways they have chosen to follow must be recognized. And since that is true, we have reason to feel and to show satisfaction in the achievements of John Dos Passos. So typical of his generation in his training and interests, so conscious of their dilemmas, so responsive to the causes of their despair, he has scorned to imitate their evasions, has known but never surrendered to their gloom, and has succeeded where they failed. Whatever place the future may grant his books, he cannot be denied the historical importance of having been a challenge to a generation that considered itself safely lost.

SUGGESTIONS FOR ADDITIONAL READING

For students who wish to familiarize themselves with more background knowledge of the 1920's, an excellent starting place is Frederick Lewis Allen's entertaining monograph, *Only Yesterday: An Informal History of the Nineteen-Twenties* (New York, 1931), a surprisingly accurate account for a work published so soon after that era ended. A more negative interpretation can be found in *Epic of America* (Boston, 1931), Historian James Truslow Adams's vinegary treatment of the so-called prosperity decade. Complementing historical studies of this period also include Preston W. Slosson, *The Great Crusade and After, 1914–1928* (New York, 1930) and James C. Malin, *The United States After the World War* (Boston, 1930). Charles Angoff, "The Tone of the Twenties," *Literary Review*, IV (Autumn, 1960), 5–15, and Frederick J. Hoffman, "The Temper of the Twenties," *Minnesota Review*, I (Fall, 1960), 36–45, offer judicious capsule accounts.

Valuable insights covering varied phases of the post-World War I era are made in Henry F. May, "Shifting Perspectives on the 1920's," *Mississippi Valley Historical Review*, XLIII (December, 1956), 405–427, and Burl Noggle, "The Twenties: A New Historiographical Frontier," *Journal of American History*, LIII (September, 1966), 299–314. These excellent essays are fortified with rich documentation. Two general collections of readings which treat many aspects of the decade are Milton Plesur (ed.), *The 1920's: Problems and Paradoxes* (Boston, 1969) and Loren Baritz (ed.), *The Culture of the Twenties* (Indianapolis and New York, 1970). Short but interpretive treatments of the 1920's are Paul Carter, *The Twenties in America* (New York, 1968) and Roderick Nash, *The Nervous Generation: American Thought, 1917–1930* (Chicago, 1970). See also John Braeman, Robert H. Bremner, David Bronx, eds., *Change and Continuity in Twentieth Century America: The 1920's* (Columbus, Ohio, 1968).

There are, of course, no substitutes for the selections contained herein. However, a wealth of scholarship touching upon America's "Lost Generation" of writers deserves careful scrutiny. An indispensable pamphlet which places the subject in its historical perspective is Henry F. May (ed.), *The Discontent of the Intellectuals: A Problem of the Twenties* (Chicago, 1963). Arthur M. Mizener, "The Lost Generation" and Richard P. Blackmur, "The American Literary Expatriate," both praise the vision of the literary exiles and are included, respectively, in Robert E. Spiller (ed.), *A Time of Harvest: American Literature, 1910–1960* (New York, 1962), 73–82, and David F. Bowers (ed.), *Foreign Influences in American Life: Essays and Critical Bibliographies* (Princeton, 1944), 126–145. "The Generation That Wasn't Lost," *College English*, V (February, 1944), 233–239, and "Twenty-Five Years After: The Lost Generation Today," *Saturday Review of Literature*, XXXIV (June 2, 1951), 6–7, 33–34, contain the well-balanced judgments of Malcolm Cowley on a problem which he believes reflected the "generation gap" of the 1920's. Cowley supplies helpful definitions throughout these essays. Also worth attention is Warren I. Susman, "A Second Country: The Expatriate Image," [University of] *Texas Studies in Literature and Language*, III (Summer, 1961), 171–183. A general cultural history of overseas expatriation, including material on the 1920's, is George Wickes, *Americans in Paris* (New York, 1969). See also Ishbel Ross, *The Expatriates* (New York, 1970).

Broader coverages of the decade's intellectual dissenters abound. For interpretations that are generally critical of those American authors who spent their *Wanderjahre* on the Continent, see Maxwell D. Geismar's two volumes, *The Last of the Provincials; The American Novel, 1915–1925: H. L. Mencken, Sinclair*

Lewis, Willa Cather, Sherwood Anderson, F. Scott Fitzgerald (Boston, 1947) and *Writers in Crisis; The American Novel, 1925–1940: Ring Lardner, Ernest Hemingway, John Dos Passos, William Faulkner, Thomas Wolfe, John Steinbeck* (New York, 1961). Sympathetic essays on some of these same authors will be found in Cowley (ed.), *After the Genteel Tradition: American Writers, 1910–1930* (Carbondale, Illinois, 1964 ed.). For a useful evaluation and comparison of post-war writers, with the clear edge given to the daring experimenters of the twenties, see Malcolm Cowley, "Two Wars—and Two Generations: The Novelist's [*sic*] Climate in the Twenties and His Legacy to the Novelist of Today," New York *Times Book Review* (July 25, 1948), 1f. The novels and the novelists of the period are given careful attention in two general studies of interest, Alfred Kazin, *On Native Grounds: An Interpretation of Modern American Prose Literature* (New York, 1942 ed.) and Joseph W. Beach, *American Fiction, 1920–1940* (New York, 1941). Edmund Wilson's *The American Earthquake: A Documentary of the Twenties and Thirties* (Garden City, New York, 1958) is a collection of helpful essays and literary reviews dealing with the inter-war years.

If "the Lost Generation" scored the corporeal mentality of the prosperity decade, its alienation experience prepared the way for its eventual reintegration into American life. Both these themes are treated respectively, in David Lewin, "The Literary Expatriate as a Social Critic of America" (Ph.D. dissertation, New York University, June, 1953) and Warren I. Susman, "Pilgrimage to Paris: The Backgrounds of American Expatriation, 1920–1934" (Ph.D. dissertation, University of Wisconsin, June, 1958). For a summary statement of the motivations of the expatriates, refer to Marion Joy Bonn, "The American Novelists of the Twenties: Their Exile and Return" (Ph.D. dissertation, Pennsylvania State University, June, 1955). Although highly specialized, James L. Colwell's "The American Experience in Berlin During the Weimar Republic" (Ph.D. dissertation, Yale University, May, 1961) is of interest.

Those who wish to delve into the matter more deeply need to consult several of the rich reminiscences of the exiles. Far and away one of the most sincere memoirs of Paris life is Van Wyck Brooks's *Days of the Phoenix: The Nineteen-Twenties I Remember* (New York, 1957). This autobiographical volume is replete with revealing sketches of the lives of the literary artists. Matching its frankness is the briefer but rambling essay of Edward Dahlberg, "The Expatriates: A Memoir," *Texas Quarterly*, VI (Summer, 1963), 50–55. Robert McAlmon's angry recollections are more than adequately balanced by the evenhanded remembrances of Kay Boyle in their *Being Geniuses Together, 1920–1930* (Garden City, New York, 1968). For a memorial which makes a searching examination of the reasons for expatriation, see Samuel Putnam, *Paris Was Our Mistress: Memoirs of a Lost and Found Generation* (New York, 1947). This memoir should be read with Gertrude Stein's "An American and France," in Philip Rahv (ed.), *Discovery of Europe: The Story of American Experience in the Old World* (Boston, 1947), 571–578, an introspective explanation of why Paris became her "home town." An intriguing testimonial by a novelist who sought solace in the American Communist Party of the 1920's is Joseph Freeman's *An American Testament: A Narrative of Rebels and Romantics* (New York, 1936). Much "lively gossip" of the Paris years is found in Mizener, *The Far Side of Paradise: A Biography of F. Scott Fitzgerald* (Boston, 1951). Ernest Hemingway's *A Movable Feast: Sketches of the Author's Life in Paris in the Twenties* (New York, 1964) is also recommended.

Profitable supplementary materials also deal in part with the subject at hand. For an exhaustive study of how Freudian psychology actually influenced select writers of the post-war decade, consult Hoffman, *Freudianism and the Literary Mind* (Baton Rouge, Louisiana, 1957). Joseph W. Krutch has written a challenging account, *The Modern*

Temper: A Study and a Confession (New York, 1929) which is quite fatalistic in tone. He believed that America's belletristic contributions were symptomatic of the general "cultural senescence" of the 1920's. Equally provocative is Max Eastman's *The Literary Mind: Its Place in an Age of Science* (New York, 1931), a collection of essays centering about the author's sceptical view of the spiritual world. The role of the literary critic during this era is adequately treated in Morton D. Zabel, *Literary Opinion in America* (New York, 1951 rev. ed.), Gorham B. Munson, "The Young Critics of the Nineteen-Twenties," *Bookman*, LXX (December, 1929), 369–373, and Granville Hicks, "The Twenties in American Literature," *Nation*, CXXX (February 12, 1930), 183–185. Also see Walter B. Rideout, *The Radical Novel in the United States, 1900–1954: Some Interrelations of Literature and Society* (Cambridge, Massachusetts, 1956), an especially valuable analysis of one hundred and seventy books which have at their root Marxian themes.

1 2 3 4 5 6 7 8 9 10